Tricycle Theatre and Shared Experience
World Premiere

BRACKEN MOOR

By Alexi Kaye Campbell

WELCOME

I am really delighted that within my first year of programming we have a new play by Alexi Kaye Campbell. When I started this job, Alexi was one of the writers that I most wanted to see on the Tricycle stage. So when Polly Teale brought me *Bracken Moor*, it was a no-brainer, to be honest. Shared Experience has a long history with the Tricycle Theatre attracting hugely loyal audiences to their shows here. But this is the very first time that the Tricycle has co-produced with Shared Experience: it's a joint venture and a new journey for both companies.

Thank you for coming and for your support.

Indhu Rubasingham
Artistic Director, Tricycle Theatre

It was while Alexi was working as an actor for Shared Experience that he wrote *The Pride*, his first produced play. I read it and was completely captivated and so we commissioned him to write a play for us. I knew immediately that there was a deep connection to the work of the company. So it feels like a homecoming for Shared Experience to be bringing *Bracken Moor* to life for the first time.

Polly Teale
Artistic Director, Shared Experience

SHARED EXPERIENCE

Shared Experience has pioneered a thrillingly distinctive performance style that celebrates the union of physical and text-based theatre.

The company is committed to creating work that goes beyond our everyday lives, taking flight into the imagination and examining the hidden parts of the self. Tackling potent universal themes, Shared Experience explores the relationship between the world we inhabit and our inner lives.

Over the years, Shared Experience has become renowned for bringing literary classics to life in bold, imaginative ways, and for developing ambitious new productions with some of today's most dynamic playwrights. Led by the award-winning writer and director Polly Teale, the company's productions place the lives of women and unheard voices centre stage.

Recent productions include *Mary Shelley*, *Brontë*, and *Speechless*, all of which toured nationwide, and, in 2007, an acclaimed production of *Kindertransport*, featuring in the cast an actor and budding playwright by the name of Alexi Kaye Campbell.

"Pushing the boat of theatricality way beyond its usual moorings"

The Guardian, on Shared Experience

The Tricycle Theatre first opened in 1980 and has established itself as one of London's most significant theatres. Today, with Indhu Rubasingham as Artistic Director, the Tricycle continues its reputation for presenting the highest quality British and international work, that reflects the diversity of its local community.

Open seven days a week, the Tricycle not only comprises a unique 235-seat theatre, but also an independent 300-seat cinema, vibrant bar and café, plus three rehearsal spaces used for creative learning and community work.

The Tricycle is committed to bringing unheard voices into the mainstream and presenting work that provokes debate and emotionally engages.

Recent productions include *Red Velvet*, which launched Indhu Rubasingham's inaugural season winning two Critics' Circle Awards and an Evening Standard Award; *The Arabian Nights*, a modern re-imagining of ancient tales for young people, Eclipse Theatre Company's entertaining revival of Don Evans' *One Monkey Don't Stop No Show*, and *Paper Dolls*, an extraordinary true story of cultures colliding in Tel Aviv.

"What an incisive, fervent beginning. Indhu Rubasingham takes over with panache at the Tricycle, bowing to the theatre's politically engaged tradition but giving it a sharp new turn."

Susannah Clapp, The Observer, 21 Oct 2012

THE ROAD TO WIGAN PIER

In 1936, George Orwell was commissioned to write an account of life in the depressed areas of the North of England. He spent two months in Lancashire and Yorkshire living amongst the people whose lives he so vividly describes.

The Road to Wigan Pier was first published in 1937, the same year in which *Bracken Moor* is set.

'Watching coal-miners at work, you realise momentarily what different universes different people inhabit. Down there where coal is dug it is a sort of world apart which one can quite easily go through life without ever hearing about. Probably a majority of people would even prefer not to hear about it. Yet it is the absolutely necessary counterpart of our world above.'

'Practically everything we do, from eating an ice to crossing the Atlantic, and from baking a loaf to writing a novel, involves the use of coal, directly or indirectly. For all the arts of peace coal is needed; if war breaks out it is needed all the more. In time of revolution the miner must go on working or the revolution must stop, for revolution as much as reaction needs coal. Whatever may be happening on the surface, the hacking and shovelling have got to continue without a pause.'

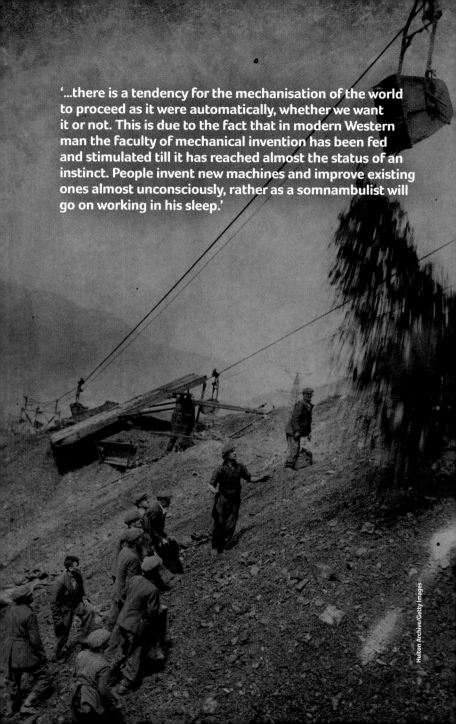

'...there is a tendency for the mechanisation of the world to proceed as it were automatically, whether we want it or not. This is due to the fact that in modern Western man the faculty of mechanical invention has been fed and stimulated till it has reached almost the status of an instinct. People invent new machines and improve existing ones almost unconsciously, rather as a somnambulist will go on working in his sleep.'

'In every country in the world the large army of scientists and technicians, with the rest of us panting at their heels, is marching along the road of 'progress' with the blind persistence of a column of ants. Comparatively few people want it not to happen, and yet it is happening. The process of mechanisation has itself become a machine, a huge glittering vehicle whirling us we are not certain where...'

Excerpts from The Road to Wigan Pier by George Orwell © 1937.

Antony Byrne Photo: Tristram Kenton

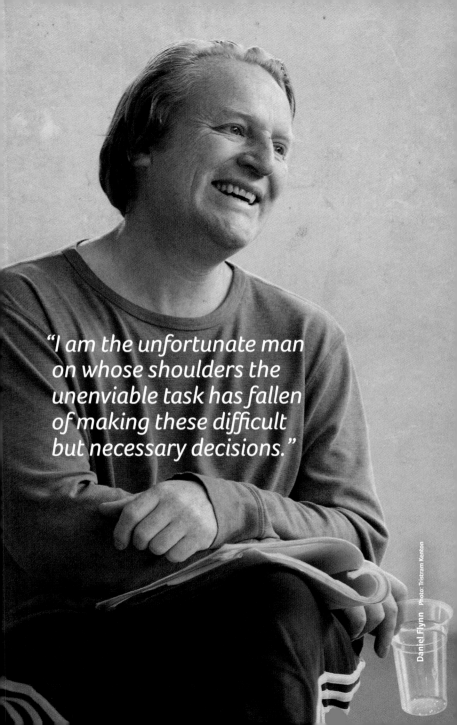

"*I am the unfortunate man on whose shoulders the unenviable task has fallen of making these difficult but necessary decisions.*"

Daniel Flynn   Photo: Tristram Kenton

World Premiere
Co-produced by Tricycle Theatre and Shared Experience

BRACKEN MOOR

By Alexi Kaye Campbell

THE COMPANY

CAST	*in alphabetical order*
John Bailey / Dr Gibbons	Antony Byrne
Harold	Daniel Flynn
Eileen	Natalie Gavin
Elizabeth	Helen Schlesinger
Geoffrey	Simon Shepherd
Terence	Joseph Timms
Vanessa	Sarah Woodward
Company	Bili Keogh and Jamie Flatters
Director	Polly Teale
Designer	Tom Piper
Lighting Designer	Oliver Fenwick
Composer and Sound Designer	Jon Nicholls
Movement Director	Liz Ranken
Production Manager	Shaz McGee
Company Stage Manager	Shannon Foster
Deputy Stage Manager	Lauren Harvey
Assistant Stage Manager	Lucy Holland
Assistant Director	Rosy Banham
Costume Supervisor	Natasha Ward
Wardrobe Assistant	Gina Rose Lee
Voice Coach	Majella Hurley
Fight Director	Ruth Cooper-Brown of Rc-Annie
Casting Director	Amy Ball
Youth Casting Director	Lotte Hines
Press Representation	Clióna Roberts
Production Photography	Tristram Kenton
Learning Resource Pack	Aisling Zambon, Rosy Banham, Anna Myers
Crew	Charlie Hayday, Andy Furby, Elz, Jonesy, Russell Martin
Wigs	Carole Hancock
Costume Makers	Nicole Small and Tony Rutherford, Eve Collins
Distressing Artist	Schultz & Wiremu Fabric Effects
Hire Costumes	Angels Costumiers
Make-up provided by	MAC
Thanks to	Daragh Moroney and his family

THE CAST

Antony Byrne
John Bailey/
Dr. Gibbons

Theatre includes:
Jane Eyre (Shared Experience); *On The Waterfront* (Theatre Royal Haymarket); *After Troy* (Oxford Playhouse, Shaw); *Wuthering Heights* (Birmingham Rep, Tour); *The Elephant Man* (Sheffield Lyceum, Tour); *Macbeth* (Regent's Park); *Skellig* (Young Vic); *Betrayal* (Peter Hall Co., Tour); *Twelfth Night* (West Yorkshire Playhouse); *Rutherford & Son* (Royal Exchange, Manchester); *Henry VIII, The Island Princess, The Roman Actor, Tales From Ovid, The Phoenician Women, The Tempest* (RSC); *The Madness Of George III* (National Theatre).

Television includes: *Law & Order: UK, Coronation Street, The Suspicions of Mr Whicher, Playing The Field, Touching Evil, Emmerdale, Prime Suspect.*

Film includes: *Anna Karenina, The Wind That Shakes The Barley, Thick As Thieves, Bathory.*

Daniel Flynn
Harold Pritchard

Theatre includes:
55 Days (Hampstead); *Richard II, Translations* (Donmar); *Emperor And Galilean, The White Guard, The Madness of George III, A Chorus Of Disapproval* (National Theatre); *Twelfth Night, Cymbeline, Camelot, A Midsummer Night's Dream, Troilus And Cressida* (Regent's Park); *Four Knights In Knaresborough, Chips With Everything, Charlie And The Chocolate Factory* (West Yorkshire Playhouse); *Alice In Wonderland, The Tempest, Bingo* (RSC); *Betrayal* (Exeter); *A Small Family Business* (Chichester); *Twelfth Night* (Crucible); T*he Winter's Tale, Anna Christie* (Young Vic); *All In The Wrong, Love's A Luxury, The Secret Life* (Orange Tree); *A Chorus Of Disapproval* (Scarborough, World Premiere); *A Man For All Seasons* (Haymarket); *The Weir* (Duke of York's); *Woman In Mind* (Vaudeville).

Television includes: *The Last Days of Anne Boleyn, Room At The Top, Vera, The Bill, After Life, Murder Room, Island At War, William & Mary, Murder In Mind, The Peter Principle, Peak Practice, Bugs, The Choir, Soldier Soldier, A Breed Of Heroes, The Detectives, Casualty, The Buddha Of Suburbia, Heidi, No Excuses, The Two Gentlemen Of Verona, Goodbye Mr Chips, The Two Of Us.*

Film includes: *Biggles.*

Natalie Gavin
Eileen Hannaway

Natalie Gavin makes her professional stage debut at the Tricycle Theatre.

Television includes: *The Syndicate* (BBC); P*risoners' Wives* (BBC); *The Chase* (BBC); *Shameless* (Channel 4).

Film includes: *The Knife That Killed Me, Jasmine, The Arbor.*

Helen Schlesinger
Elizabeth Pritchard

Theatre includes: *The Mill On The Floss* (Tricycle/Shared Experience); *War And Peace* (National Theatre/Shared Experience); *Fireface* (Young Vic); *Skane, Comfort Me With Apples* (Hampstead); *Blue/Orange* (Arcola); *The Gods Weep* (Hampstead/RSC); *The Stone, Wild East, The Weather, Bear Hug* (Royal Court); *Whipping It Up* (Bush, Ambassadors); *The Crucible* (Gielgud/RSC); *The Oresteia, An Inspector Calls, Inadmissable Evidence* (National Theatre); *Twelfth Night, The Merchant Of Venice* (RSC); *Uncle Vanya, King Lear, Moon For The Misbegotten* (Royal Exchange, Manchester).

Television includes: *Eastenders, Merlin, Criminal Justice, The Way We Live Now* (BBC); *Nativity, Trial And Retribution, Sensitive Skin* (ITV).

Film includes: *Dirty War, 24 Hour Party People, Persuasion.*

Simon Shepherd
Geoffrey Avery

Theatre includes: *Posh* (Royal Court, Duke of York's); *Bent* (Royal Court); *Art, Secret Rapture, A Tale Of Two Cities, The Browning Version* (West End); *Dracula, Romeo And Juliet* (Lyric Hammersmith); *Born In The Gardens* (Peter Hall Season, Bath); *Our Man In Havana* (Nottingham Playhouse); *Coram Boy, Ghosts, The Seagull, Betrayal* (Bristol Old Vic); *Painter's Palace of Pleasure* (Citizen's Theatre, Glasgow).

Television includes: *Touch Of Frost, Heartbeat, Invisibles, Poirot, Warriors, Bliss, Peak Practice, Gimme Gimme Gimme, Miss Marple, Kisko: A Life For A Life, Tilly Trotter, Beyond Reason, Ruth Rendell Mysteries, Aubrey Beardsley,Chancer.*

Film includes: *Frail, Carmen, Rogue Trader, Wuthering Heights, Insatiable Mrs Kirsch, Henry V.*

Joseph Timms
Terence Avery

Theatre includes: *Privates On Parade* (Noël Coward); *The Taming of the Shrew* (Shakespeare's Globe); *Someone Who'll Watch Over Me* (Southwark Playhouse); *Richard II* (Donmar); *Twelfth Night* (National Theatre); *Bedlam, Henry IV Part 1 & 2* (Shakespeare's Globe).

Television includes: *Doctors, Casualty.*

Radio includes: *A Midsummer Night's Dream* (BBC Radio 4).

Sarah Woodward
Vanessa Avery

Theatre includes: *Love And Information, Jumpy, Presence* (Royal Court); *The Cherry Orchard, Present Laughter, The Hour We Knew Nothing Of Each Other, Wild Oats, The Sea* (National Theatre); *Snake In The Grass* (Print Room); *The Merry Wives Of Windsor, The Comedy of Errors, Much Ado About Nothing* (Shakespeare's Globe); *Judgment Day, Venus & Adonis* (Almeida); *Rookery Nook* (Menier Chocolate Factory); *A Midsummer Night's Dream, Macbeth, Romeo & Juliet, Arms & The Man* (Regent's Park); *Habeas Corpus* (Donmar); *The Real Thing* (Donmar, West End, Broadway); *Tom & Clem*: Olivier Award For Best Supporting Actress (Aldwych); *The Tempest; Venetian Twins, Murder In The Cathedral, Love's Labour's Lost, Henry V, Hamlet, Richard III, Camille* (RSC); *Woman In Mind* (Salisbury Playhouse).

Television includes: *Outnumbered, The Prime Minister's Husband, Loving Miss Hatto, DCI Banks, Law & Order, Doctors, Kingdom, New Tricks, The Bill, Final Demand, Hear The Silence, Inspector Pitt Mysteries, Poirot, Casualty.*

Film includes: *I Capture The Castle, Bright Young Things, Close Your Eyes, The House Of Angelo.*

"But even when I looked into the mirror, you stared back at me."

Helen Schlesinger Photo: Tristram Kenton

"The force of habit. I think most of us are walking around in a sort of slumber really."

Simon Shepherd

CREATIVES

Alexi Kaye Campbell
Writer

Alexi's first play, *The Pride*, premiered at the Royal Court Theatre Upstairs in November 2008 for which he won the Critics' Circle Award for Most Promising Playwright and the John Whiting Award for Best New Play. The production was also awarded the Olivier Award for Outstanding Achievement in an Affiliate Theatre.

His second play, *Apologia*, was on at the Bush Theatre. It was short-listed for The John Whiting Award and nominated for Best Play at the Writers' Guild Awards 2009.

Alexi's third play, *The Faith Machine*, premiered at the Royal Court Theatre in August 2011.

Polly Teale
Director

Polly Teale has created a unique body of work as a writer and director that has won critical and audience acclaim with productions transferring to the West End and touring internationally. She is Artistic Director of Shared Experience and has authored a number of original plays and stage adaptations, including *Jane Eyre*, *Brontë*, and *After Mrs Rochester* for which she won the Evening Standard Award for Best Director and the Time Out Award for Best West End Production.

Other directing credits include: *Mary Shelley*, *Speechless* (co-writer/director), *The Glass Menagerie*, *Mine* (writer/director), *Ten Tiny Toes*, *Kindertransport*, *Madame Bovary*, *The Clearing*, *A Doll's House*, *The House of Bernarda Alba*, *Desire Under the Elms*, and, as co-director, *War and Peace* (co-production with National Theatre) and *The Mill on the Floss*.

Her play *Brontë* has inspired a screenplay that is in pre-production with Pathé.

Alexi Kaye Campbell   Photo: Tristram Kenton

Tom Piper
Designer

Forthcoming designs include: Costume designs for *Pride And Prejudice* and *A Winter's Tale* (Regent's Park); *Antony and Cleopatra* (RSC).

Tom is the Associate Designer of the RSC. His recent work there includes *Boris Godunov, Much Ado About Nothing, Macbeth* and *City Madam, The Histories Cycle* (Courtyard, Roundhouse); designing *Richard II, Henry IV – Parts 1 & 2, Henry V, Henry VI – Parts 1, 2 & 3* and *Richard III* for which he won the 2009 Olivier Award for Best Costume Design and was nominated for the 2009 Olivier Award for Best Set Design, *As You Like It, The Grain Store, The Drunks* and *Antony And Cleopatra.*

Other recent designs include: *Red Velvet* (Tricycle); *Goodbye To All That, Vera, Vera, Vera* (Royal Court, Theatre Local); *King Lear* (Citizen's Theatre); *Richard III, The Tempest, As You Like It* (Bridge Project at BAM, Old Vic); *Zorro* (West End, Tour, Paris, Moscow, Amsterdam, Tokyo, Atlanta); *Dealer's Choice* (Menier Chocolate Factory, West End); *Falstaff* (Scottish Opera); *Fall* (RSC at the Traverse); *Spyski* (Lyric Hammersmith, Tour); *The Scarecrow And His Servant* (Southwark Playhouse); *Plough And The Stars, The Crucible, Six Characters In Search Of An Author* (Abbey, Dublin).

Oliver Fenwick
Lighting Designer

Theatre includes: *Paper Dolls, Red Velvet, Poison, The Caretaker* (Tricycle); *The Holy Rosenbergs, Happy Now?* (National Theatre); *The Witness, Disconnect* (Royal Court); *My City, Ruined* (Almeida); *The Winter's Tale, The Taming Of The Shrew, Julius Caesar, The Drunks, The Grain Store* (RSC); *Berenice, Huis Clos* (Donmar); *After Miss Julie* (Young Vic); *Saved, A Midsummer Night's Dream* (Lyric, Hammersmith); *To Kill A Mockingbird, The Beggar's Opera* (Regent's Park); *The Madness Of George III, Ghosts, Kean, The Solid Gold Cadillac, Secret Rapture* (West End); *A Number* (Menier Chocolate Factory); *Private Lives, The Giant, Glass Eels, Comfort Me With Apples* (Hampstead Theatre); *Hamlet, Comedy Of Errors* (Crucible, Sheffield).

Jon Nicholls
Composer and Sound Designer

Theatre includes: *Spring Storm, Beyond The Horizon, The Holy Rosenbergs* (National); *Who's Afraid Of Virginia Woolf?* (Crucible); *Yerma* (Gate); *The Norman Conquests* (Liverpool); *Red Light Winter, In The Next Room, The Welsh Boy, Deadkidsongs, The Double* (Theatre Royal Bath); *Blue Remembered Hills, Art, The Changeling, Silas Marner* (Theatr Clwyd); *Katherine Desouza, The Mothership* (Birmingham Rep); *Rutherford & Son* (Northern Stage); *Eden End, Humble Boy, The Prime of Miss Jean Brodie, In Praise of Love, A Midsummer Night's Dream, Dancing At Lughnasa* (Royal & Derngate Northampton).

Opera includes: *Falling Across, Flicker.*

Jon has worked on numerous TV documentaries and extensively in music and sound design for radio drama.

Liz Ranken
Movement Director

Liz has a long-standing relationship with Shared Experience, having worked on many of the company's productions. She is a founder member of DV8, Associate Movement Director at the RSC and has worked extensively with Dominic Cooke. She is the winner of the 1992 Dance Umbrella Time Out Award, The Place Portfolio Choreographic Award (Artists to Invest In) and a Capital Award at the Edinburgh Fringe Festival. Liz is an associate artist for the RSC and her painting of Michael Boyd has been taken into the RSC portrait collection and has been recorded in the archive at the National Portrait Gallery.

"I think of him often. Perhaps I've forgotten the shape of his eyes, the sound of his voice, even though a part of me yearns to remember them. But he is a presence in my life, always somewhere near me."

"Perhaps what has happened has something to do with that part of his mind that isn't fully conscious."

Natalie Gavin Photo: Tristram Kenton

SHARED EXPERIENCE

YOUR SUPPORT NOW WILL MAKE THE DIFFERENCE

- **30 years of changing the landscape of British theatre**
- **★★★★★ productions**
- **Seen by thousands of people across the UK and abroad**
- **Led by one of the UK's foremost directors**
- **Nurturing new writers, actors and theatre-makers**
- **Inspiring audiences of all ages**

Over the years, Shared Experience has become renowned for bringing literary classics to life in bold, imaginative ways, and for developing ambitious new productions with some of today's most dynamic playwrights. The company's unexpected loss of its core Arts Council funding shocked the arts world when it became headline news in 2011:

"It's as if one of the theatre's most beautiful children had been kicked in the teeth." Frank McGuinness

Since then, Shared Experience has completed its move to Oxford Playhouse, where it is now Resident Company. This partnership has provided it with a secure footing on which to build and the company is quickly rising to the challenge of securing its future.

However, without core funding, every production needs your support. If you have ever considered making a donation to support the great theatre Shared Experience produces, now would be a perfect time: from £1 – £50,000 every penny counts.

Donate online via **www.sharedexperience.org.uk**

Alternatively, to find out how you can make a difference, email **supportus@sharedexperience.org.uk**

SHARED EXPERIENCE: 30 YEARS OF GROUND-BREAKING THEATRE

LEARNING

Shared Experience is a recommended practitioner on the AQA syllabus. The education team offers workshops and theatre events to support all Shared Experience productions, through which students are able to gain a deeper understanding of the company's unique rehearsal process. Two-hour workshops are available for Drama and English Literature students for ages 14+ and can be tailored for groups studying at GCSE, A-Level or Higher Education levels.

A *Bracken Moor* Resource Pack is available to download FREE from our website at www.sharedexperience.org.uk

FOR SHARED EXPERIENCE

Artistic Director	Polly Teale
Producer	Michelle Walker
Producer's Assistant	Hannah Bevan
General Management	Oxford Playhouse
Marketing	Richard Matthews, Erin McDonald, Russell Souch, Lisa Sullivan, Bethan James

BOARD OF DIRECTORS
Chair: Richard Humphreys
Olga Edridge
Charlotte Partridge
Alistair Petrie
Alan Rivett
Mary Roscoe

GUARDIAN ANGELS
Joan Bakewell
Nica Burns
Nancy Meckler

HONORARY CHAMPIONS
George Carey
Clare Lawrence Moody

Shared Experience is Resident Company at Oxford Playhouse, whose programme includes the best of British and international drama, family shows, contemporary dance and music, student and amateur performance, comedy, lectures and poetry. www.oxfordplayhouse.com

SHARED EXPERIENCE
Oxford Playhouse, Beaumont Street, Oxford OX1 2LW
T: 01865 305321 sharedexperience.org.uk

 /sharedexperience   @setheatre

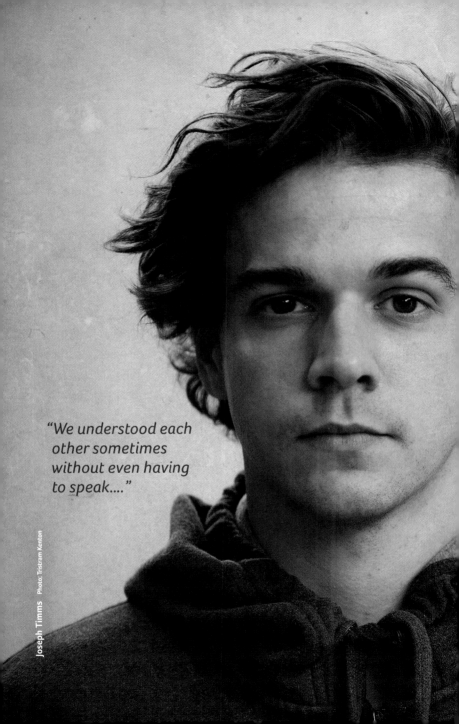

"*We understood each other sometimes without even having to speak....*"

Joseph Timms Photo: Tristram Kenton

The Tricycle Theatre has always been a pioneer and a risk-taker. As we herald a new chapter, your support will help us to continue this bold tradition during uncertain economic times. Individuals, grant-making trusts and corporate partners play a vital role in supporting our ambitious artistic programme and creative learning work with young people in the local community.

'We believe deeply in all the work it does both artistically and educationally'

Primrose and David Bell, Tricycle members since 1996

With your support

- We can continue to push boundaries artistically across stage and screen, building on the success of productions such as the critically acclaimed and award-winning *Red Velvet* and *The Great Game: Afghanistan*.

- We can extend the reach of our creative learning programmes, inspiring a new generation of audiences and providing young theatre-makers with a professional context in which to develop their skills, aspirations and potential.

Join us today

'I like the atmosphere, like supporting the values of the Tricycle, and enjoy coming with friends.'

Steven Baruch, Tricycle member since 2004

Our members receive the very best benefits across stage and screen, with invitations to member events, priority booking, and opportunities to observe our creative learning work. Membership starts from just **£125** per year. To join and for further details, please visit www.tricycle.co.uk, phone the Development Department on **020 7625 0132** or email **development@tricycle.co.uk**.

Thank you in advance for your support.

THANK YOU

We are extremely grateful to our supporters, whose help has made the work we produce at the Tricycle Theatre possible year after year. Thank you for your support.

PUBLIC FUNDING

TRUSTS & FOUNDATIONS

    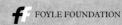

AB Charitable Trust
Ardwick Charitable Trust
Aspect Charitable Trust
Austin & Hope Pilkington Trust
Barcapel Foundation
The Bertha Foundation
Brown-Mellows Trust
Catkin Pussywillow Charitable Trust
95.8 Capital FM's Help a Capital Child
Concertina Charitable Trust
The Coutts Charitable Trust
D'Oyly Carte Charitable Trust
John Ellerman Foundation
Esmée Fairbairn Foundation

Equity Charitable Trust
Garfield Weston Foundation
Garrick Charitable Trust
Robert Gavron Charitable Trust
J. Paul Getty Jr. Charitable Trust
The Goldsmiths' Company
Guildford Academics Association
The Ernest Hecht Charitable Foundation
Government of Ireland
Irish Youth Foundation
Kobler Trust
Little Charity
John Lyon's Charity
The MacArthur Foundation

Mackintosh Foundation
David & Elaine Potter Foundation
Sigrid Rausing Trust
The Henry Smith Charity
Sir Siegmund Warburg Voluntary Settlement
The Sobell Foundation
The Stanley Foundation
The Topinambour Trust
Vanderbilt Family Foundation
Harold Hyam Wingate Foundation
The Worshipful Company of International Bankers

INDIVIDUALS

Major Donors
Noralee & Jon Sedmak
Jonathan & Lucy Silver
Al & Joan Weil
Joseph & Sarah Zarfaty

Director's Circle
Sir Trevor & Lady Susan Chinn

Pioneers
Liz Astaire
Gillian Frumkin
John Reiss
Jonathan Tyler
Joseph & Sarah Zarfaty

THANK YOU

Front Wheels
David & Jenny Altschuler
Primrose & David Bell
Jennie Bland
Helen & Keith Bolderson
Katie Bradford
Fiona Calnan
Kay Ellen Consolver
   & John Storkerson
Frankie de Freitas
Lady Hatch
Sir Christopher Hogg
Sarah Ingham
Miki Jablkowska
Anya & Grant Jones
Judy Lever
Jeremy Lewison
   & Caroline Schuck
Andrée Molyneux
Diana & Allan Morgenthau
Peter Roth
Michael & Gail Sandler
Professor Philippe Sands
Marjorie & Albert Scardino
Carol Sellars

Innovators
Henry Chu & James Baer
Noreen Doyle
Posgate Charitable Trust
Rajeev Samaranayake
Professor Aubrey Sheiham

Benefactors
Helen Fraser
Tony & Melanie Henderson
John & Margaret Mann
Jackie Rothenberg

Supporters
David & Francine Altaras
Steven & Sharon Baruch
Debbie Behrens
Mr & Mrs Binstock
Martin Blackburn
Kenneth E Brown
Jules Burns
Mary Callaghan
James Carroll & Dycella
Cummings-Palmer
Mrs L Colchester
Lily & Anthony Filer
Sue Fletcher
Sybil Goldfoot

Rosita & Brian Green
Martyn Gregory
Peter Guter
Barbara Hosking
Christine Jackson
Stephen Jellis
Christopher Knowles
   & Mary Anne Bonney
David Lanch
Isabelle Laurent
Simon & Pauline Malpas
Liz Marsh
Geoff Mayne
Lyn Meadows
Ruth & Paul Miller
Jim Minton
Michael & Jenny Nathan
Dr & Mrs Papadakis
I G & B Rappaport
Michael Robinson
Dr Joan Schachter
Christine Scholes
Brian Smith
Pauline Swindells
Mrs Tynan
Judith Farbey & Prabhat Vaze
Lavinia Webb
Ros & David Wright

The Tricycle would also like to thank the Friends, Trailblazers and all anonymous donors

Cinema Box Members
Steven & Sharon Baruch
David Cohen
Veronica Cohen
Gerry & Kim Davis
Fiona Finlay
Jack Gold
Bird & Alan Hovell
Gillian Howard
Anna Jansz

Ann & Gerard Kieran
Christopher Kitching
Jenifer Landor
Monique Law
John & Rose Lebor
Isabel Martorell
M P Moran & Sons Ltd
Terry Munyard
Gina Newson
Catherine Roe

John & Melanie Roseveare
Philip Saville
Glenis Scadding
Isabelle & Ivor Seddon
Barrie Tankel
Emma Thompson
Eliana Tomkins
Maggie Turp
Sandar Warshal and Family
Christine & Tom Whiteside

Opportunities for corporate partnership include production sponsorship, funding a creative learning workshop, joining as a corporate member or supporting another element of the Tricycle's work on stage or screen, with benefits for both the company and staff. Please contact the Development Department on 020 7625 0132 for further details.

CORPORATE PARTNERS

Bloomberg

The Clancy Group PLC
Daniel & Harris Solicitors
J. Leon & Company Ltd
JPC Law
London Walks Ltd
Mulberry House School
The North London Tavern
Samuel French Ltd

We are enormously grateful to the members of our Development Committee, who volunteer their expertise and experience by advising on and supporting the Tricycle's fundraising activities.

Kay Ellen Consolver (Co-Chair); Judy Lever (Co-Chair); Lesley Adams; Nadhim Ahmed; Baz Bamigboye; Andrew Daniel; Sally Doganis; Kobna Holdbrook-Smith; Grant Jones; Mairead Keohane; Jonathan Levy; Jeremy Lewison; Anneke Mendelsohn; Andree Molyneux; Allan Morgenthau; Michael Sandler; Christine Scholes; Caroline Schuck; Geraldine Sharpe-Newton; Sue Summers

The Tricycle Theatre was founded by Shirley Barrie and Ken Chubb.
The Tricycle Theatre Company Ltd. Registered Charity number 276892.

Registered Office: 269 Kilburn High Road, NW6 7JR
Administration: 020 7372 6611 Box Office: 020 7328 1000 Fax: 020 7328 0795
Email: info@tricycle.co.uk

FOR THE TRICYCLE

Artistic Director
Indhu Rubasingham
Executive Director
Kate Devey
Executive Producer
Bridget Kalloushi
Technical Director
Shaz McGee
Artistic Associate
Nic Wass
Associate Producer
Zoe Ingenhaag
Marketing Director
Holly Conneely
Senior Marketing Officer
Alice Wright
Marketing Assistant
Ben Carruthers
Development Manager
Lisa Morlidge
Development
Liam Fisher Jones
Administrative Manager
Trish McElhill
Creative Learning Director
Mark Londesborough
Creative Learning Managers
Mary Chilton
Anna Myers
Finance Officers
Lise Bell
Jane Pollendine
Cinema Programmer
John Morgan Tamosunas
Projectionist
Michael Rose
Relief Projectionist
S R Gobin
Archivist (Voluntary)
Anne Greig

FRONT OF HOUSE

Business Manager
Gail Deacon
House Managers
James Foran, Andy Orme,
Owen Sampson
Relief House Managers
James Bush, Paul Carstairs,
Tara Kane, Michael O'Kelly,
Elliot Taylor
Box Office Manager
Tom Nolan
**Assistant Box Office
Manager**
Emma Faulkner
Box Office Supervisors
Michael Byrne,
Joanna Beattie
Front of House Team
Tolu Alaka-Babatunde
Jeremy Fowler
David Porter
Maks Andala
Jennifer Majka
Olivia Armstrong Long
Mary Guerin
Joshua Manning
Enrico Aurigemma
Steve Hines
Caitlin Hoskins
David Stroud
Simona Bitmaté
Chris Hughes
Tara Stroud
Miles Brown
Tariq Jordan
Ben Victor
Jessica Clark
Emma Kizintas

Niamh Webb
Leah Cox
Alice Lee
Alex Williams
Keiron Craven-Grew
Danielle Nott
Emily Mae Winters
Jane Crawshaw
Hillary Pierce
Siobhan Witter
Daniel Essongo
Clare Pointing
Jasmine Yoloye
Rodolphe Fleury
Francesco Ponzo
David Porter

Cleaners
Theresa Desmond,
Dominic O'Connor,
Joslette Williamson

Board of Directors
Baz Bamigboye, Fiona
Calnan, Kay Ellen Consolver,
Barbara Harrison, Pam
Jordan, Jenny Jules, Judy
Lever, Jonathan Levy (Chair),
Jeremy Lewison, Philippe
Sands, Lady Simone Warner

**Brent Council
Representatives**
Cllr Ann John/Cllr Mary
Arnold, Cllr Reg Colwill

Accountants
Jon Catty and Company
Insurance Brokers
Walton & Parkinson Ltd

Creative Associates: Lolita Chakrabarti, Adrian Lester and Rosa Maggiora

/TricycleTheatre @TricycleTheatre www.tricycle.co.uk

Alexi Kaye Campbell

BRACKEN MOOR

NICK HERN BOOKS
www.nickhernbooks.co.uk

SHARED EXPERIENCE
www.sharedexperience.org.uk

TRICYCLE THEATRE
www.tricycle.co.uk

Bracken Moor was first performed at the Tricycle Theatre, London, in a co-production between Shared Experience and the Tricycle Theatre, on 6 June 2013, with the following cast:

JOHN BAILEY/DR GIBBONS	Antony Byrne
HAROLD	Daniel Flynn
EILEEN	Natalie Gavin
ELIZABETH	Helen Schlesinger
GEOFFREY	Simon Shepherd
TERENCE	Joseph Timms
VANESSA	Sarah Woodward
COMPANY	Bili Keogh & Jamie Flatters

Director	Polly Teale
Designer	Tom Piper
Lighting Designer	Oliver Fenwick
Composer & Sound Designer	Jon Nicholls
Movement Director	Liz Ranken

For Angie

Acknowledgements

With thanks to Juliet Gardiner, Rosemary Preece at the National Coal Mining Museum, Susie Sainsbury, and everyone at the National Theatre Studio.

Alexi Kaye Campbell

We must go down into the dungeons of the heart,
To the dark places where modern mind imprisons
All that is not defined and thought apart.
We must let out the terrible creative visions.

Return to the most human, nothing less
Will teach the angry spirit, the bewildered heart,
The torn mind, to accept the whole of its duress,
And pierced with anguish, at last act for love.

May Sarton, 1912–1995

8

Characters

EDGAR PRITCHARD, *twelve*
JOHN BAILEY, *fifties*
HAROLD PRITCHARD, *late forties/early fifties*
EILEEN HANNAWAY, *early twenties*
TERENCE AVERY, *twenty-two*
VANESSA AVERY, *late forties*
GEOFFREY AVERY, *fifties*
ELIZABETH PRITCHARD, *late forties*
DR GIBBONS, *fifties*

The parts of John Bailey and Dr Gibbons should be played by the same actor.

The play takes place entirely in the drawing room of the Pritchards' home on the hills overlooking a mining village in Yorkshire in December 1937.

This text went to press before the end of rehearsals and so may differ slightly from the play as performed.

With the house lights still up, the actors playing HAROLD *and* JOHN *walk on stage. The actor playing* HAROLD *is carrying his shoes, not wearing them. He sits in a chair and puts them on, tying the laces. He then stands and buttons up his waistcoat.*

Meanwhile, the actor playing JOHN *stands in front of a mirror which happens to be positioned somewhere on stage as part of the set and combs his hair.*

We watch the ritual of two actors in the last moments of preparation before a performance. Then, when their checks are complete, they both take their starting positions and look at each other as if to confirm that they are now both ready for the play to begin.

Blackout.

We can hear EDGAR's *voice but we can't see him. The voice of an anguished child in the dark.*

EDGAR. Mother? Father?

Pause.

Mother, where are you? Father. Father!

Pause.

Mother, Father, please. I'm scared.

Pause.

Please, Father, please!

Pause.

Mother. Father. Where are you?

ACT ONE

Scene One

Lights up.

The drawing room of the Pritchards' home in Yorkshire. This is the main room in a grand old house of an affluent, land-owning family. It is a large, imposing room that announces wealth but not great style. It is masculine and somewhat oppressive in its dark hues and in its scale. The furniture too is heavy and graceless though undoubtedly expensive. The overall impression is one of formality but little joy; as if, in some way, the house has become unloved over the years.

It is an evening in December 1937.

HAROLD PRITCHARD *stands in the middle of the room. He is a man of magnetic and intimidating presence – handsome in an austere way and confident with the knowledge of his position in the world. He is smartly dressed.*

Opposite him stands JOHN BAILEY, *a well-built man who speaks in a strong Yorkshire accent and is wearing a well-worn suit and overcoat that have been exposed to the elements.*

JOHN. I urge you to reconsider.

Pause.

If we let Ramshaw Drift go – if you decide to close it – the village will be decimated.

Pause.

There is no alternative work – nothing left for these men to do. And they have given their best – as have their fathers and their fathers' fathers before them – to help make this industry the proudest Britain has to offer. But of course you know this already, sir, it is not my business to educate you on the matter, merely to remind you of the necessity to reflect on their dedication over the years and on our duty to honour it.

HAROLD. And you do so to great effect, Mr Bailey.

JOHN. Only because I have lived with these people, Mr
    Pritchard, I am one of them.

HAROLD. Indeed you are.

JOHN. I have known their toil and I recognise them by the
    sweat of their brow, the strength of their hands and their
    knowledge of the land.

HAROLD. You are becoming poetical.

JOHN. It is not a pretence, sir. If I speak with some passion it is
    only because I feel what I say.

HAROLD. I do not doubt your sincerity, Mr Bailey, I only
    question the way you are using language in order to
    persuade. And in that effort at least, it may prove to be a
    waste of your creative endeavours. I'm afraid the situation
    demands less poetry and more pragmatism; those,
    unfortunately, are the times in which we live.

JOHN. I stopped by Ramshaw Drift on my way here, sir. There
    was a problem with one of the cutters – the one I mentioned
    to you last week, do you remember? – and so I needed to
    inspect it and ascertain that it was in working order once
    again, which indeed it was.

HAROLD. Well, that's reassuring.

JOHN. And as I was leaving I noticed Alfie Shaw walking
    homewards. His shift had just finished and I caught sight of
    him by the edge of the road and asked him if he wanted a lift
    in the motor.

HAROLD. Good man.

JOHN. Alfie Shaw, sir – he was the red-haired lad who
    impressed us all a couple of autumns ago when he helped
    pull out that poor boy who broke his leg on his very first day.
    Brought him out on his shoulders like an Achilles.

HAROLD. And now you are invoking mythology.

JOHN. So I drove him to his cottage and he asked me in for a
    quick brew. I wouldn't usually have taken the time, Mr
    Pritchard, only I was keen not to give offence and made

myself promise that it would be a quick one and as I wasn't
expected here till six and a half o'clock I scurried in for a
cup of tea.

HAROLD. You did well, Mr Bailey.

JOHN. And it was then that I remembered that Alfie Shaw was
recently widowed. His young wife – a pretty thing she was
though always weak in constitution – succumbed to
consumption a year or so ago, not a day older than twenty-
five, I'm sure. And as I'm having my tea I notice something
moving around in the corner of my eye and in the doorway I
catch three little girls – seven, five and three years of age I'd
guess and pretty things all of them with their father's
strawberry hair and his freckles too but thin like their
mother, nay, more than thin, skin and bones, Mr Pritchard,
skin and bones.

HAROLD. You are painting an evocative picture, Mr Bailey,
but to what purpose? I must compel you to reach your point,
I have guests who have just arrived from London and so my
time is pressured.

JOHN. Skin and bones even with their father working and his
mother, old Mrs Shaw helping him out no doubt though
that's another mouth to feed and the girls' eyes full of hope
and worry but there I was sitting in that cold house
wondering, Mr Pritchard, what will become of them if you
should go ahead and take his job from Alfie Shaw and
another one hundred and forty men like him, what should
become of those poor, helpless creatures standing in the
doorway.

Pause. HAROLD *moves over to the drinks cabinet and
pours himself a Scotch.*

HAROLD. Do you read the papers, Mr Bailey?

JOHN. When I have the time, Mr Pritchard, when I have the
time.

HAROLD. Of course. But you have, I assume, over the last few
months caught enough of a glimpse of them to formulate an
impression of what I would call, the bigger picture?

JOHN. And what would the bigger picture be, sir?

HAROLD. The one, Mr Bailey, which often contradicts our more sentimental natures.

JOHN. Does it indeed?

HAROLD. But which we have to heed in order to survive. Not only as individuals but as communities and nations. And which now dictates that sacrifices need to be made.

JOHN. On that we are both agreed, Mr Pritchard.

HAROLD. Good.

JOHN. What we may not be in agreement about is the nature of the sacrifices that are demanded and who they are demanded of.

HAROLD. You are aware, Mr Bailey, that our country – indeed most of the civilised world – is only now beginning to emerge from the worst economic crisis it has ever known.

JOHN. So they say.

HAROLD. But that our industry – the one we have both given our lives to for better or worse, continues to be one of the main casualties of this crisis.

JOHN. I am aware of the challenges we all face.

HAROLD. Demand is down by fifteen per cent this year, Mr Bailey, and that is not my doing.

Surely you have heard that the Fitzwilliams have recently let more than two thousand of their men go – not a mere one hundred and forty but *two thousand*, Mr Bailey – in a concerted effort to keep the business going.

JOHN. To keep their costs down, sir, yes.

HAROLD. These are hard times, Mr Bailey, and so perhaps you need the clarity of mind to comprehend that closing Ramshaw Drift for a few years until demand picks up again is not a strange fancy of mine. I am simply the unfortunate man on whose shoulders the unenviable task has fallen of making these difficult but necessary decisions and believe me when I say that I gain little enjoyment from it.

JOHN. But there is an alternative.

Pause.

You may call me presumptuous but I have been working hard at trying to find it and I think I may have finally stumbled upon it.

HAROLD. Working hard at what, my man?

JOHN *hurriedly takes out a few sheets of paper from his inside pocket.*

JOHN. I was up all night thrashing ideas about and putting some of them in writing. But the solution I think I have arrived at will mean that we can hold on to those men whilst only marginally affecting the profits.

HAROLD. My guests will be down at any moment, Mr Bailey.

JOHN. It is to do with the forthcoming purchase of the new conveyors for the Hook Hill mine. I do believe that they haven't been paid for yet. I spoke to Mr Milson, the accountant and he informed me that this was the case. He implied that should it all go to plan the transaction should proceed at some point next week and that the whole thing had been delayed because of the late arrival of some of the machinery from America.

HAROLD. You had no business talking to Mr Milson, sir.

JOHN. Of course I understand the positive contribution that this advanced technology will have on the efficacy of the mines in general, speeding up the whole process of extraction.

HAROLD. That is the intention, yes.

JOHN. But if perhaps we could postpone this investment for another two years we could keep the men in full employment whilst not severely compromising the quantity of our output.

HAROLD. And how would that be possible, Mr Bailey?

JOHN. Close Ramshaw Drift if you have to, Mr Pritchard, but re-employ the men – all one hundred and forty of them at nine shillings a shift – two less than what they are currently earning – on only five shifts each at Hook Hill. Those extra shifts will help speed up the output without resorting to the

new conveyors and if my calculations are precise the damage
to the profit margin will be minimal, perhaps a few hundred
short per annum.

HAROLD. Is that all?

JOHN. I've spoken to the men and they all without exception
agreed to take the cut in wages and shifts as a means of
holding on to their employment. I also called a meeting with
the miners who are already employed at Hook Hill and they
are willing to lose a shift each a week in order to help their
colleagues from Ramshaw Drift hold on to their jobs.

HAROLD. I begin to see why you are not a man of business,
Mr Bailey.

JOHN. So really I suppose what I am suggesting is that you
deliberately delay the acquisition of the new conveyors until
perhaps a more appropriate time. Perhaps when things are
looking a little brighter and the demand picks up again.

HAROLD. You're asking me to delay progress.

JOHN. Only perhaps to broaden the definition of that word.

HAROLD. My dear man, I honestly applaud the noble nature of
your enterprise and the zeal with which you have just
communicated it. Alfie Shaw and the other men have a
champion in you, there's no denying.

JOHN. I am doing my duty by them, that's all.

HAROLD. But perhaps they would be better served by someone
with fewer ideals and just a little more common sense.

JOHN. I am simply asking you –

HAROLD. You would rather I kept my business securely
fastened to archaic methods thus making it wholly
uncompetitive and in the long run jeopardising the jobs of
many more than a hundred and forty.

JOHN. I repeat, sir, that productivity will not be compromised.
The men will work fewer shifts for less money that is all.

HAROLD. You are asking me to sabotage my business in order
to quench a sentimental yearning and dare I say it aspirations
towards some type of moral heroism.

JOHN. Those are not my motives, I assure you.

HAROLD. Thank you for sharing your scheme with me and I only wish I could say I will give it serious consideration.

JOHN. And so I return to your point about the sacrifices that need to be made in these challenging days, Mr Pritchard.

HAROLD. But the irrationality of its premise excludes the possibility of me taking it with any seriousness at all.

JOHN. And venture to suggest something quite radical: that the sacrifices are not demanded of those who have nothing left to sacrifice.

HAROLD. We are finished, Mr Bailey. I suggest you return to your duties.

There is a knock at the door and EILEEN *enters.*

EILEEN. Oh, I do beg your pardon, sir, I didn't realise Mr Bailey was here.

HAROLD. Mr Bailey is on his way out, Eileen, so your timing is convenient, no need to apologise.

EILEEN. I've shown Mr and Mrs Avery to their rooms, sir, and young Mr Avery too and asked them to join you for drinks when they're ready.

HAROLD. Thank you, Eileen. And you best notify Mrs Pritchard of their arrival.

EILEEN. I shall, sir.

HAROLD. Goodbye, Mr Bailey, Eileen will show you out.

EILEEN. Follow me, Mr Bailey.

JOHN. Don't worry yourself, Miss Hannaway, I know my own way out. Mr Pritchard.

He leaves the room, followed by EILEEN. HAROLD *is left alone in thought.* TERENCE *enters. He is a striking young man, handsome in an unusual way, and charismatic.*

HAROLD *has his back to him so doesn't immediately notice him, which allows* TERENCE *to study him for a few seconds. But then* HAROLD *senses him and turns.*

HAROLD. Good grief.

TERENCE. I'm sorry, I didn't mean to startle you.

HAROLD. Hovering there like a ghost.

TERENCE. I do apologise.

HAROLD. You're Terence I presume?

TERENCE. Mr Pritchard, how d'you do?

He comes forward and shakes his hand.

HAROLD. You've changed.

TERENCE. Have I ?

HAROLD. You're not a child any more.

TERENCE. I'm twenty-two years of age.

HAROLD. Last time I saw you you were…

TERENCE. Just a boy, yes. Twelve years old to be exact. It's been ten years.

HAROLD. And what are you up to, young man? I do believe my wife mentioned that you were at Merton.

TERENCE. That's not quite accurate, sir. I mean I was, but I left.

HAROLD. You've graduated?

TERENCE. Not quite, sir. I decided to leave at the end of my second year. I found Oxford stifling if truth be told.

HAROLD. How do you mean you left?

TERENCE. And embarked on travelling to the East. Constantinople initially and then onwards to Greece from whence I've just returned. I've just spent three months of perfect solitude in the monastic retreat of Mount Athos.

HAROLD. And what do you plan to do with your life now? Sit around in London smoking a hookah pipe and reminiscing?

TERENCE. I haven't decided yet, sir, but I'm not one for sitting around for too long. But writing is my forte or at least my passion.

HAROLD. Writing what exactly?

TERENCE. Well I was commissioned by *The Burlington* to do a piece on Byzantine icons which is one of the reasons I travelled to the places I did. So I'm writing about those.

HAROLD. A writer then. An aesthete too?

TERENCE. I don't know if I'm that. The word aesthete at least to me suggests a certain type of decadence. Beauty and art are all very well but I believe they have a role to play other than sating the pleasure of the one who either creates or dwells on them.

HAROLD. What kind of role?

TERENCE. I'm more interested in their transformative qualities.

HAROLD. And what would they be?

TERENCE. Qualities which move one towards one's higher purpose, I suppose.

HAROLD. So you're religious as well are you?

TERENCE. Call it what you will, sir. I simply believe that the way we're living our lives and the social structures we have adopted are not the only possible ones. In a matter of fact I suspect that they don't represent our real capabilities to any extent at all.

HAROLD. What are our real capabilities then, young man?

TERENCE. I'm sure we'll find out in due time. A little mystery is a good thing when it's married to a little patience.

HAROLD. You speak in riddles.

TERENCE. I'm just trying to answer your questions.

HAROLD. You're not a damned Bolshevik are you?

TERENCE. I hope you're not offended when I say you're awfully keen on labels, sir.

HAROLD. Why shouldn't I be? They let you know what or whom you're dealing with.

TERENCE. As long as they're accurate I suppose.

HAROLD. I'm usually right in my impressions of people.

TERENCE. Or if you're not I expect you're very convincing at persuading yourself that you are.

HAROLD. You're a forward young man aren't you?

TERENCE. I do beg your pardon if I seem rude, sir. I don't mean to be.

HAROLD. And so what does the future hold?

TERENCE. We'll have to wait and see.

HAROLD. Your plans I mean. Schemes. Ambitions.

TERENCE. I'm not a locomotive, sir. My feet are not attached to any sort of track.

HAROLD. Standing on the platform are you?

TERENCE. I believe it's a good thing to know what exactly one is hurrying towards before one actually commences the hurrying.

HAROLD. I'm a hard-working man and the one thing I have learnt is that introspection is merely an excuse for indolence.

TERENCE. Surely that depends on the quality of the introspection.

HAROLD. And then of course you'll have to get yourself a good wife to help you on your way.

TERENCE. I'm not sure I'm the marrying kind.

HAROLD. Rubbish. Every man's the marrying kind.

TERENCE. Are they?

Pause. He holds his stare for a beat.

HAROLD. Will you have a drink with me?

TERENCE. I'll have whatever you're having, sir.

HAROLD *goes to the drinks cabinet and pours him a Scotch.*

HAROLD. Do you remember the house at all?

TERENCE. I do, yes.

HAROLD. Ten years is a long time.

TERENCE. And I remember the grounds as well. I remember playing in them. There's a brook if I'm not mistaken at the back of the garden. And beyond it an entire hill covered in heather.

HAROLD. More than one.

TERENCE. We used to... I remember playing there.

HAROLD. With my son.

TERENCE. Yes, sir, with Edgar.

HAROLD. You got on the two of you, didn't you?

TERENCE. Famously, yes.

HAROLD. That's right.

TERENCE. We seemed to understand each other instinctively. I think it would be fair to say in hindsight that Edgar was the best friend I ever had.

HAROLD. That made my wife very happy.

TERENCE. He was a kind boy I remember with a very wicked sense of humour.

HAROLD. Yes, yes, little devil.

TERENCE. We understood each other sometimes without even having to speak.

Pause. HAROLD *hands* TERENCE *his drink.*

Can I ask you something?

HAROLD. Ask away.

TERENCE. The bedroom I'm in. It looks familiar. It's his, isn't it? Edgar's I mean.

HAROLD. We've closed down the east wing for repairs so apart from the one your parents are in it was the only one we had left. You don't mind?

TERENCE. Not at all. If anything, I quite like it. It makes me feel rather close to him.

HAROLD. What a peculiar thing to say.

TERENCE. But I wasn't sure my memory served me well. The room looked familiar but all his… the objects have all been cleared.

HAROLD. One must keep looking forward.

VANESSA AVERY *enters, followed by her husband* GEOFFREY.

VANESSA. Oh my dear Harold, we've arrived at last.

HAROLD. Hello, Vanessa. Geoffrey.

GEOFFREY. You haven't aged a day, you rascal.

HAROLD. All the fresh air I imagine.

VANESSA. Where is she, where is she, where is she.

HAROLD. The girl's gone to tell her you arrived, I assume she'll be down in a couple of minutes. Hello, Vanessa.

They kiss.

VANESSA. Oh, we had the most ghastly time getting here, my dear.

HAROLD. I'm sorry to hear it.

GEOFFREY. Bloody awful actually.

VANESSA. Well, eventful at the very least.

HAROLD. What will you have?

VANESSA. Any old spirit to calm the nerves. Do you have sherry?

HAROLD. One sherry for Vanessa and for Geoffrey?

GEOFFREY. I'll have a Scotch, old man. And quickly.

HAROLD *pours them their drinks*.

VANESSA. First we were forced to share a compartment up to Stevenage with this awful woman who kept going on about how Herr Hitler was the best thing that's happened to Europe in a hundred years. Geoffrey didn't even contradict her.

GEOFFREY. She wouldn't let me get a word in edgeways.

VANESSA. Kept going on and on about how we were going to see the light and join forces with him and what she meant by that I'm really not quite sure. Invade the world I imagine.

GEOFFREY. She had a moustache very like his, perhaps that was what inspired the affinity.

VANESSA. Terence kept giving her the strangest looks didn't you, darling?

TERENCE. Did I?

VANESSA. As though she belonged to a whole different species.

TERENCE. I think she did.

GEOFFREY. She had a point about the show he put on for the Olympics though. Rather impressive it was, all those straight lines and things, very inspiring.

VANESSA. And then afterwards on the second leg of the journey we absolutely froze, the train felt positively Siberian.

GEOFFREY. And it just juddered to a grinding halt for half an hour somewhere outside Wakefield.

VANESSA. Then when we got off at Leeds the damned wind grabbed hold of my hat and threw it straight into the path of the Edinburgh train.

GEOFFREY. I told you to hold on to it. But thank you for sending your man to pick us up anyway.

HAROLD. I'm sorry you had such a time of it.

VANESSA. Oh, but it's worth it, Harold, every single mile of the way.

GEOFFREY. It's definitely worth it.

VANESSA. To be here again. To be here.

She suddenly begins to weep.

Oh, I'm so sorry, I'm so dreadfully, dreadfully, sorry. I'm being a complete fool.

GEOFFREY. What's got into you?

VANESSA. I'm ever so sorry, I really don't know. Probably just tiredness. That and the excitement of seeing my dearest friend after a whole ten years.

TERENCE. It's understandable, Mother.

VANESSA. You've been keeping her locked up, Harold, you brute.

HAROLD. I've done no such thing.

VANESSA. Not a single trip to London in ten years. And for four of them she didn't even answer my letters, I've been sick with worry.

GEOFFREY. I would imagine it's natural after all that happened.

HAROLD. But now she's ready to emerge again.

VANESSA. Like a butterfly from its chrysalis.

HAROLD. I wouldn't go that far. Tentatively, and with small steps.

VANESSA. I almost jumped with joy when I received her letter. I've missed her dreadfully. And she was so keen to see Terence too.

HAROLD. It was my idea, I won't lie to you. Not that I had to apply too much pressure once I suggested it. But I think it's time we tried to resuscitate her a little if you know what I mean.

VANESSA. Well, rest assured, you've called the right people for the job.

HAROLD. But a word of caution if I may.

Pause.

She's not the woman you knew, Vanessa.

VANESSA. I'm not expecting her to be.

HAROLD. And so you might need to acclimatise yourself as it were. She hasn't really left the house in years. And her moods tend towards the morbid.

GEOFFREY. Morbid?

VANESSA. Well, we'll do our best to cheer her up won't we, boys?

GEOFFREY. Our very best.

ELIZABETH *enters but nobody sees her, and for a while she stands framed in the doorway. She is a beautiful woman but sombre in her appearance – both her clothes and her expression are of a dark shade.*

VANESSA. I remember before you married her, Harold, and dragged her off up here she was the life of the party, wasn't she, Geoffrey? Most of London was absolutely seduced by her and she had a number of impressive suitors, not least that French count with the high-pitched voice and a penchant for miniature dogs.

GEOFFREY. Something tells me that union wouldn't have led to much conjugal bliss.

VANESSA. And then when your father died and you inherited this place you both decamped here and apart from the odd holiday we lost you for ever. God knows what drove you to it. Trying to avoid people like us most probably.

HAROLD. There was work to be done, Vanessa. I wasn't going to stay in the bank for ever. Someone had to run the land, and the pits.

VANESSA. And all of a sudden she was gone. But she was a beauty and much admired.

ELIZABETH. Hello, Vanessa. Hello, Geoffrey.

They all turn and see her.

VANESSA. Oh my dear, darling girl.

ELIZABETH. Yes, those were the days weren't they, Vanessa? Carefree and idle and gay.

VANESSA. My dear, dear girl.

VANESSA *runs up to her and embraces her.* ELIZABETH *returns the embrace but is much more held back.*

ELIZABETH. Parties and parties and more parties even though the war had just ended and the stench of it still hovered over everything. Hello, Geoffrey.

GEOFFREY. Hello, my darling.

ELIZABETH. So we'd leave our boys with their nannies and party through the night. As if all those poor souls who had perished under the ground, in the darkness and the fear were just an inconvenience to be forgotten.

VANESSA. We were doing our best to live our young lives.

ELIZABETH. Is that what we were doing?

Pause.

HAROLD. Come and sit down, darling, there's a good girl.

ELIZABETH. I think I'll stand.

She turns to VANESSA *and* GEOFFREY.

Thank you for coming. It's a long way I know.

VANESSA. I'd have travelled to China and back to see you again, my dear.

ELIZABETH. It means a lot to me that you made the effort. It gets lonely up here, especially when the days get short doesn't it, Harold?

She suddenly sees TERENCE.

Terence.

TERENCE. Hello, Mrs Pritchard.

ELIZABETH. Terence.

She goes up to him.

What a beautiful boy you are.

HAROLD. He's a man, Elizabeth, not a boy any more.

ELIZABETH. You haven't changed have you? I'd have recognised you anywhere.

HAROLD. I said the opposite.

TERENCE. It's lovely to see you again, Mrs Pritchard.

ELIZABETH. My Edgar loved you so.

HAROLD. Darling.

ELIZABETH. 'Mummy, he's the best friend I ever had' he used to say 'and he understands me better than I do myself.' Isn't that an extraordinary thing for a boy of twelve to say?

VANESSA. Very.

ELIZABETH. But then he was an extraordinary boy wasn't he, Vanessa?

VANESSA. He was, my darling.

ELIZABETH. Well, you both were, Terence.

Pause.

Welcome back.

TERENCE. Thank you, Mrs Pritchard. I'm happy to be here.

HAROLD. Right, enough of all this, where's that stupid girl, she needs to tell Cook we'll be eating in an hour.

He rings a bell.

And I'll pour you a drink. Gin?

ELIZABETH. Thank you, Harold, I'll do it myself.

She moves over to the drinks cabinet and pours herself a gin on the rocks.

I'm sorry I've changed so much since you last saw me, Terence. I've become rather an old lady before my time haven't I? So forgive me if my appearance comes as something of a shock.

TERENCE. You look beautiful, Mrs Pritchard, and I'm the forgiving type anyway.

VANESSA. Oh, he is, aren't you, darling, and open-minded and tolerant and all those things.

HAROLD. And so are you by the sound of it, Geoffrey.

GEOFFREY. Am I?

HAROLD. Hardly raising an eyebrow when he pulls out of his studies to go gallivanting round the world.

GEOFFREY. He's his own man, no use trying to stop him.

TERENCE. Mr Pritchard wasn't very keen on me exploring the East.

HAROLD. Or the Arctic Ocean or the Amazon. Travelling is all very well in times of leisure but leisure is the one thing we can't afford at the moment. This country needs to whip itself back into shape.

GEOFFREY. Hear, hear.

HAROLD. Only this week I'm having to let a hundred and forty men go. So to be passing one's times traipsing around the Balkans hardly seems to me like the right priority at this particular moment. Our young men should be here at home making the most of themselves and offering the best they have.

ELIZABETH. Harold enjoys lecturing people and he hasn't had much of a chance lately so to have a young man in the house is an opportunity he can't pass by.

TERENCE. Surely in times of crisis it's a good thing to look at things from further away, sir, as well as reflect a little on where we've come from as a means of perhaps forging the path ahead with some due thought.

HAROLD. And where is it you think we've come from?

TERENCE. I only refer to that particular part of the world where the mystic and the rational first conjoined forces in forming the roots of our civilisation.

HAROLD. So you returned from your travels a fan of the Eastern Mediterranean did you, young man? Did you especially admire their politics or their sewage systems?

TERENCE. It is true that when it comes to plumbing our role as world leaders in the field is incontestable.

VANESSA. Do we really need to discuss plumbing and sewage before dinner?

TERENCE. Not only plumbing mind you; our contribution to all aspects of technology – to science in all its forms is unmatched and admirable, no question about that. I am almost willing to bet that one day soon we will be flying to the Moon and planting a Union Jack on it, another far-fetched corner of the Empire.

GEOFFREY. Oh, the Americans will get there first, they're a pushy bunch.

VANESSA. And brash too like that awful Simpson creature.

TERENCE. But how sad it will be and pathetic if we do it all in the wrong order.

HAROLD. What 'wrong order'?

TERENCE. If we proudly land on the Moon and have all these machines announcing our prowess and the shining brilliance of human intelligence when we still live in a world that is scarred by inequality and riddled with poverty and ignorance.

HAROLD. Good God I was right, your son's a Red. I'm surprised you haven't packed your bags to join Orwell and all those other Commies in Spain yet.

VANESSA. He's an idealist that's all and a passionate one at that.

TERENCE. I simply think that somewhere along the way, as we were busy building machines we didn't notice that the world we were living in began to resemble those very machines.

GEOFFREY. Hold on, you've lost me, what machines?

TERENCE. And so the machines took over and meanwhile they had robbed us of some of the better things that made us human to begin with, the best of our natures and our imaginations. As well as our more mystical side.

HAROLD. Stuff and nonsense, young man. 'Mystical side' indeed – backward superstition and mumbo-jumbo.

GEOFFREY. Easy does it, old man, he's just young.

HAROLD. Well, I've never heard such a load of rubbish, is that the expansive education you picked up on your travels around the world? If it is God help us, I'm more worried about the next generation than I was to begin with. Is that what we fought the war for, Geoffrey?

He rings the bell again, more aggressively.

TERENCE. I'm not saying it's one without the other or a choice between the two. Machines are wonderful things that make our lives a whole lot better, you'd be an idiot to disagree.

HAROLD. My point exactly.

TERENCE. But why should we allow a machine, or an economic system that works like a machine to dictate everything to us at great cost to that strange thing we call the human soul?

HAROLD. Because there is no viable alternative.

TERENCE. I would suggest, sir, with some caution that that statement indicates a distinct lack of imagination.

GEOFFREY. Easy, Terence.

TERENCE. And surely this is the best opportunity – now that the machine seems to have temporarily broken down – to ask ourselves the most fundamental questions on whether it has been working to our best advantage and with our well-being as its priority. Otherwise I fear history will keep repeating itself and the results will eventually prove catastrophic.

HAROLD. And now you have become a prophet of doom.

TERENCE. No, rest assured, sir, I haven't such an important opinion of myself. It was just that you asked me what we could learn from the East and I suppose my answer is that perhaps humility would be a good quality for us to cultivate.

HAROLD. A few months away, Geoffrey, and your son's spouting a whole lot of dangerous hogwash, I'd keep an eye on him if I were you.

GEOFFREY. What do I know, I'm just a bloody shopkeeper.

VANESSA. Don't talk yourself down. You're an antiques dealer and the best one in London.

The door opens and EILEEN *enters in a state of distress.*

HAROLD. Where the hell have you been? I've been ringing for ages.

EILEEN. Oh, sir, madam, I do beg your pardon, the strangest thing.

ELIZABETH. What's wrong, Eileen? You look ashen.

EILEEN. I was up in… I was upstairs unpacking young Mr Avery's case –

TERENCE. You needn't do that, I can do it myself after dinner.

EILEEN. Oh, it's no trouble, sir, no trouble at all, but I had just finished and I'd put away all your shirts, sir, and everything else too, folded them all away in the little cupboard and placed the case under the bed so that it isn't in the way and I turned off the light and walked out into the corridor but then I remembered I'd forgotten the towels for the bathroom on the bed so I started to make my way back into the room and then… and then…

HAROLD. And then what?

EILEEN. I pushed the door and it was jammed, sir. I mean it wasn't locked or anything because it was ajar like so much, a couple of inches or so, but when I pushed to open it wouldn't budge, like someone else was standing on the other side and pushing it towards me and this went on and on and I thought perhaps someone was playing a joke on me or something but it still wouldn't open and then eventually, a whole minute later, all of a sudden the pressure from the other side stopped and it swung open and I nearly fell to the ground with the force of it.

HAROLD. So what's all the fuss about, you silly girl. It was a draft, you know what it's like up there.

EILEEN. Oh, but, sir, but it wasn't a draft, I could have sworn there was somebody pushing it on the other side.

HAROLD. For God's sake, we were all down here so it wasn't any of us and unless Cook suddenly decided to abandon preparing the lamb in order to terrorise you with a ridiculous prank the likelihood is it was a powerful gust of wind.

EILEEN. Oh, but, sir, I swear on my mother's –

HAROLD. Anyway, enough of that. Tell Cook we'll be having dinner at eight as planned.

EILEEN. Yes, sir.

She makes a move to go.

ELIZABETH. It's all right, Eileen. I know it wasn't a draft or a gust of wind. I understand.

EILEEN. Yes, ma'am. Thank you, ma'am.

She goes.

HAROLD. The girl's an hysteric, always has been.

Pause.

GEOFFREY. Now you two ladies will want to do some catching up. Ten years is a hell of a long time.

HAROLD. Tell you what, why don't we men go into my study for a cigar and leave you to do a little chatting on your own?

GEOFFREY. What a winning idea.

VANESSA. A cigar before dinner? Are you sure?

GEOFFREY. Of course we're sure.

HAROLD. And then we'll all convene for Cook's leg of lamb.

VANESSA. You don't have to. We can catch up later can't we, Elizabeth.

GEOFFREY. Now's a good time to start.

HAROLD. Only if your son promises to keep his progressive ideas to himself.

GEOFFREY. I can't make my son promise a thing.

TERENCE. As long as I'm not provoked you have my word, sir.

HAROLD. Come on then, follow me.

VANESSA. Off you go then.

The men leave the room and the women are left alone. For a few seconds there is an awkward silence.

So, here we are.

ELIZABETH. Yes, here we are.

VANESSA. Oh, my darling, I don't know where to start. Ten years is a lifetime.

ELIZABETH. A lifetime, yes.

VANESSA. But the most important thing is that here we are
now and we can pick things up again as if nothing at all has
happened.

ELIZABETH. As if nothing has happened?

VANESSA. What I mean is we can resume our friendship and
slowly start to do things again and how wonderful it would
be if you did get out of this place for a little while and you
got onto that train and came down to London and we could
all get together again, the whole pack of us and Milly
Hughes and the Bedford sisters and all of us again like old
times and we could go to the Café Royal and have those
lethal cocktails, wouldn't that be fun?

ELIZABETH. Yes, maybe.

VANESSA. But here we are again, the two of us, the best of
friends.

ELIZABETH. Yes.

Pause.

Only trouble is, my darling, I don't know how long I'll be
around for.

VANESSA. You're not planning to emigrate are you?

ELIZABETH. You see I had to keep going didn't I? For Harold
really. For better or worse, that sort of thing. But you know, I
think he'll be fine. His work keeps him going, he doesn't
dwell on things like I do. So he'll be all right when I'm gone,
I'm sure of it.

VANESSA. Gone where, my sweet?

ELIZABETH. And now I think the time is coming.

VANESSA. What time? My darling, what are you talking
about?

ELIZABETH. Do you know he's like a lover that I call every
night?

VANESSA. Harold is?

ELIZABETH. No, darling, not Harold. I lie in bed at night and open myself up and I whisper, 'Come on, come on, I'm waiting for you, come and take me away, my love, take me with you, I'm all yours.' And so I call him every night into the stillness of my bedroom and into the coldness of my sheets.

VANESSA. Darling, who on earth do you mean?

ELIZABETH. Death, of course.

VANESSA. Oh, my dear girl, what a terrible thing to say.

ELIZABETH. Is it?

VANESSA. What a dreadful, dreadful thing to say.

ELIZABETH. But surely being such good friends means being honest with one another. Or is it just talking of trivial things that constitutes a friendship?

VANESSA. Elizabeth.

ELIZABETH. Oh, don't worry I shan't kill myself, that would be too cruel. No, I just know that soon my body will become host to some illness, a cancer will grow in me like a black flower or perhaps my lungs will fill up with fluid and slowly drown me but whatever it is I know he'll carry me away because I've begged him so.

Pause. VANESSA *suddenly stands.*

VANESSA. This really won't do. I won't tolerate it, I simply won't.

ELIZABETH. I do beg your pardon.

VANESSA. And of course you've been to hell and back, God knows you have and I'm the first to feel that with you because I love you so, to *commiserate* with you, to sympathise and feel with the things you have –

ELIZABETH. Thank you, Vanessa.

VANESSA. But there's a time for mourning, my darling, and then there's a time for returning and maybe that's what I'm here for.

ELIZABETH. For returning to what?

VANESSA. To life, Elizabeth, to *life*.

Pause.

ELIZABETH. All right then, you win, I'm beginning to get rather excited. Tell me how it is you plan to return me to life, Vanessa.

VANESSA. Well, darling, I'm sorry but I do think the rooms one passes one's days in have such power and influence over our moods, wouldn't you say?

ELIZABETH. Most definitely.

VANESSA. The colours and shades and – well, the overall *atmosphere* really – and I'm sorry to say this and you'll think me insensitive but, my dear girl, this house of yours really does need some cheering up.

ELIZABETH. So you think we need new furniture?

VANESSA. Well, what I was going to suggest – dear me, Harold is going to want my head on a platter for coming up with this – but what I was going to suggest is that I send you someone.

ELIZABETH. Send me someone?

VANESSA. There's this man – he's a genius, he really is – and he's just done up the Sebagos' place in Eaton Square and you've never seen anything like it. I'm sure he's terribly booked up but a phone call won't do any harm at all and we did get on, I sat next to him when Clarissa had her fortieth. He calls himself Hubert De Carcasson though Clarissa says his real name is Reginald and he's from Northampton. But anyway, the things he does with colours and fabrics – the man's a magician. He found these curtains for the Sebagos' and – it sounds hideous I know but they're absolutely beautiful – well, they have pineapples on them.

ELIZABETH. Pineapples?

VANESSA. Yes, my darling, can you believe it, these massive, fat pineapples. And I know that sounds awfully vulgar but do you know they're completely gorgeous and the room is so much fun.

ELIZABETH. I'm sure it is. Do you think we should get pineapples on our curtains here as well?

VANESSA. Well, I wouldn't go that far but all I'm saying is you could do with a little of that up here. Reg De Carcasson could work wonders. Maybe not pineapples but butterflies or something and a more joyful colour like yellow or pink or even –

ELIZABETH. A bright, shining orange. Yes, that would be nice. And butterflies is a good idea. Or rainbows or palm trees or little white seashells, and we can fill the room with cushions too and Persian rugs and maybe in the corner there we can place a fountain and people can come up from London, all those foolish, empty people and we can stand in this room holding cocktails and saying witty things to each other and laughing at one another's jokes and reminding ourselves how brilliant our lives are and so full of mirth and meaning.

Pause.

My son died, Vanessa.

VANESSA. Oh, my darling sweet angel, I know that.

ELIZABETH. And you come here and talk to me of curtains and plans to return me to life. As if that were possible. My son died.

VANESSA. I know, my darling. Ten years ago.

ELIZABETH. Oh, as long ago as that is it? Silly me, I thought it was only a few weeks. I really should pull myself together.

VANESSA. That isn't what I meant. All I was trying –

ELIZABETH. I really should try and cheer up because it's been a whole ten years. I wonder if my difficulty in pasting a smile on my face and getting on with things in the appropriate way has less to do with the fact that he actually died and more to do with the manner in which he did so. Which do you think it is, Vanessa?

VANESSA. Oh, Elizabeth, don't.

ELIZABETH. The way in which he died is what I mean, Vanessa, the *manner* of his death.

VANESSA. I know how he died, my sweet.

ELIZABETH. Do you though? Because perhaps I need to tell you. Perhaps you haven't heard the details of my son's demise.

VANESSA. No, my darling, please.

ELIZABETH. Because there have been times when I've thought that if my boy had breathed his last in his warm bed with his mother – with me, his mother – holding his hand, whispering comforting words to see him on his way, well then yes, maybe things would be a trifle easier, and maybe after a whole ten years had passed I would be able to sit here with you and discuss various types of curtains and whether we should have pineapples or butterflies or God knows what on them –

VANESSA. Please, Elizabeth.

ELIZABETH. But the simple fact is, Vanessa, that he didn't die at home with his mother kissing his brow. He died at Bracken Moor.

VANESSA. I know. I know he did.

Pause.

ELIZABETH. He used to love roaming the whole area but we never thought he'd go as far as that. You see he always used to play these imaginary games and he'd get carried away.

VANESSA. I know he did. Sometimes with Terence.

ELIZABETH. Yes, when you'd come and visit us on holidays.

VANESSA. We'd only just left.

ELIZABETH. Only the day before. Maybe that's why he'd ventured a little further on that particular morning, he was feeling sad. Maybe that's what took him to Bracken Moor.

VANESSA. Oh, my dear.

ELIZABETH. There used to be a mine there. It's been closed for years and years, since the 1870s I think.

VANESSA. Yes.

ELIZABETH. And then I suppose the bracken grew and grew and some of it grew over that one shaft.

VANESSA. It's too terrible.

ELIZABETH. Harold had a theory that some of the boys from the village had been playing there and had removed the cover. Anyway, how it happened I suppose is irrelevant really. The point is my boy fell into that mine and it was there he died.

VANESSA. The angel.

The door opens and TERENCE *walks in. They don't notice him and he remains in the corner of the room without interrupting.*

ELIZABETH. It was a shallow mine and it wasn't the fall that killed him. He'd broken his legs you see. That's why he couldn't climb out again. I bet he'd tried and tried, they found so much earth under his nails and they said that it was because he'd been fighting his way out, clawing and scratching and digging his way out like some poor little animal in the dark. He was a fighter you know, our Edgar, tough and determined even though you wouldn't know it looking at him.

VANESSA. I know he was.

ELIZABETH. But I suppose there's only so much fighting a boy can do before despair sets in.

VANESSA. Yes.

ELIZABETH. He'd never gone into that direction. So we were busy scouring to the south and the west, with me at the front of the search party, the only woman, and my voice grew hoarse from all the shouting.

VANESSA. I'm sure.

ELIZABETH. 'Edgar, my Edgar, where are you?'

VANESSA. Don't, Elizabeth.

ELIZABETH. And then when we found him a few days later his little body was limp and cold and lifeless.

Pause.

Do you know, Vanessa, they say that it took our Lord Jesus Christ nine hours to die on the cross? Well, it took my Edgar longer than three days to die in that hole. And he was frightened of the dark even though his father chided him for it. Three days of terror and anguish and pain. Three days of wondering why his parents hadn't found him yet.

Pause.

So you see, my dear, I lie in bed at night and bid death come and find me.

TERENCE *coughs a little and moves into the room.*

TERENCE. I'm sorry.

VANESSA. Oh, darling, there you are, have you all smoked your cigars and put the world to rights?

TERENCE. I wouldn't go that far. We did touch on the subject of Mr Gandhi and I rather held back but I'm afraid Mr Pritchard wouldn't even meet me halfway. He branded the man a charlatan and a nuisance and even suggested assassination.

ELIZABETH. His opinions are very fixed.

TERENCE. Anyway, I've been asked to summon you both to dinner. The lamb is done apparently.

ELIZABETH. Thank you, Terence.

VANESSA. Do you know, I'm feeling rather a chill. I think I'll fetch my cardigan.

ELIZABETH. We can send Eileen to find it.

VANESSA. Oh, don't worry her, she'll be busy getting ready to serve dinner. It'll only take me a minute.

ELIZABETH. All right then, we'll see you in the dining room.

VANESSA. Yes, yes, all right.

She leaves.

ELIZABETH. You heard some of that didn't you?

TERENCE. Just a little.

ELIZABETH. It's fine, there's no reason why you shouldn't. After all, I think you're the only person in the house who'd ever really understand.

TERENCE. Yes.

ELIZABETH. The depth of loss, I mean. The infinite depth.

TERENCE. I know what you mean, Mrs Pritchard.

Pause.

ELIZABETH. Call me Elizabeth. You don't have to if you don't want to. Not in front of the others. Only when we're alone if you like. After all, we're both adults now.

TERENCE. All right.

ELIZABETH. And he loved you so.

TERENCE. And I loved him.

Pause.

I think of him often, Elizabeth. Perhaps I've forgotten the shape of his eyes, the sound of his voice – perhaps I've forgotten these things even though a part of me yearns to remember them. But he is a presence in my life, always somewhere near me. And I think of his spirit and I think of his suffering, Elizabeth.

Pause.

ELIZABETH. He calls me sometimes.

TERENCE. Calls you.

ELIZABETH. A small voice. Usually in the dark hours of the morning.

TERENCE. Yes.

ELIZABETH. Of course I'm not going to tell Harold. He thinks me mad enough as it is. But he calls me.

TERENCE. I believe you.

ELIZABETH. 'Mummy,' he cries. 'Where are you? Come and find me.'

Pause.

We'd better go in to dinner or they'll send a search party.

TERENCE. We'd better.

ELIZABETH. We don't want to alarm them.

TERENCE. Certainly not.

She stands to go but stops.

ELIZABETH. Terence, can I ask you a favour?

TERENCE. What is it, Elizabeth?

ELIZABETH. It'll sound ever so queer but I really need to.

TERENCE. Go on then.

ELIZABETH. Hold me. Put your arms around me like you used to put them round your mother when you were a little boy and hold me.

TERENCE. Of course. Of course I will.

Slowly, tentatively, he steps forward and carefully wraps his arms around her.

The lights fade to darkness.

Scene Two

The middle of the night, a few days later. It is very windy, with a storm raging outside and the windows rattling from time to time.

All the lights are off and the stage is in darkness.

Then suddenly, the silence is pierced by a loud, terrifying scream. A few seconds pass and then EILEEN runs into the room in her nightie, and in obvious distress at the sound of the scream. She nervously tries to decide whether she should go upstairs to investigate or stay in the room and away from the danger.

A few seconds later, there is a second scream, even more piercing than the first. EILEEN is terrified and, crossing herself, she runs out of the room, muttering inaudibly as she does so and closing the door behind her.

Muffled voices are heard from upstairs, and footsteps too. The footsteps are heard rushing down the stairs and the voices too, but now they are audible. The hall light goes on outside the door.

TERENCE (*offstage*). I'm so sorry, I really am, I don't know what came over me.

ELIZABETH (*offstage*). Don't apologise, it isn't your fault, you must have had a nightmare.

The door opens and TERENCE *bursts into the room, followed by* ELIZABETH. *They are both in dressing gowns and slippers.* TERENCE *is in a distressed state.*

TERENCE. There was this thing, not so much a nightmare, more a feeling, unlike anything I've ever experienced before and then all I remember is waking up in the pitch black and I didn't know *who* I was any more, it was as if I was someone else. And then I felt this overwhelming terror and I heard this stomach-churning scream and it took me a few seconds to realise that the person who was screaming was me.

Pause.

I'm so sorry, what an appalling house guest I am, waking you up in the middle of the night like a raging lunatic.

ELIZABETH. Don't be foolish, Terence, you can't help it, these things happen.

TERENCE. But I've never experienced anything like it.

ELIZABETH. You said it was as if you weren't yourself.

TERENCE. Yes, that's exactly what it felt like.

ELIZABETH. Well, who were you then?

TERENCE. I really don't know. But it was terrifying. As if the walls had collapsed.

ELIZABETH. What walls?

TERENCE. *My* walls. I don't know. The walls that keep me safe, that make me Terence. It was as if, in that second that I woke up, I wasn't Terence at all but some poor, desperate creature who had always lived and was doomed to live eternally in the darkness.

VANESSA *rushes in, closely followed by* GEOFFREY. *They too are in their dressing gowns.*

VANESSA. Oh, my dears, what was that terrible noise?

ELIZABETH. Terence woke up in a state of terror.

VANESSA. Darling, what happened?

TERENCE. I'm awfully embarrassed.

GEOFFREY. Some sort of a nightmare, my boy?

TERENCE. More than that, but yes, a nightmare is the most accurate word to describe it I suppose.

VANESSA. That's three nights in a row now.

GEOFFREY. What is?

VANESSA. Well, we got here on Tuesday and you've had some sort of nightmare every night. And at breakfast yesterday you mentioned that thing with the whispering.

ELIZABETH. What whispering?

TERENCE. It doesn't really matter.

VANESSA. He said that he woke up with a start because –

TERENCE. It's really not important, Mother, let's leave it.

ELIZABETH. No, tell me, what whispering, what happened?

GEOFFREY. Maybe it was all that Stilton after pudding.

TERENCE. Nothing really, I was half-asleep so I must have dreamt that as well.

ELIZABETH. Dreamt what?

VANESSA. He said he heard a voice whispering in the dark, didn't you, darling? My skin crawled when you told me about it at breakfast.

ELIZABETH. What did the whisper say?

TERENCE. I imagined it, that's all. But it wasn't really saying anything in particular, it was indiscernible really, like the whisper –

ELIZABETH. Of a child?

HAROLD *comes in, also in his dressing gown and slippers.*

HAROLD. What on earth is going on?

VANESSA. Everything's fine, we can go back to bed now.

HAROLD. What happened?

GEOFFREY. Our Terence had a bit of a turn I'm afraid.

HAROLD. What kind of a turn?

TERENCE. We really should go back to bed you know and I'm sorry about the theatrics. How very dramatic, I feel a right imbecile.

HAROLD. It's four o'clock in the morning.

TERENCE. All I can repeat is that it's never happened to me before and I can only wish it never does again.

HAROLD. What hasn't?

ELIZABETH. He said it was as if he wasn't himself. As if he had become someone else.

VANESSA. That's a little worrying.

GEOFFREY. I'd keep that to yourself if I were you, people have been sent to Bedlam for less than that.

HAROLD. Not himself?

TERENCE. Anyway, really, I insist we all return to bed. If I'd known I was going to cause this much commotion I'd have stayed in my room.

VANESSA. And then we would have thought you were murdered or something.

TERENCE. In the morning we'll have forgotten all about it.

GEOFFREY. And no more cheese for you after dinner.

VANESSA. Oh, Geoffrey, do stop going on about the cheese, it has nothing to do with it.

HAROLD. Off we go then. See if we can get a couple of hours more. Elizabeth.

ELIZABETH. Yes.

They start to move towards the door. ELIZABETH *first, followed by* HAROLD *and then* VANESSA *and* GEOFFREY. TERENCE *hovers in the background.*

TERENCE. Betsy.

They all stop, turn around, and look at him. ELIZABETH*'s face changes, as if she's seen a ghost.*

That was it. That was the name. It's all coming back.

HAROLD. What is?

TERENCE. Before I screamed. When I had that feeling – that strange sensation – that I was somebody else, this name kept coming to me and I must have spoken it. 'Betsy.' I think I said it over and over again. 'Betsy, Betsy, Betsy.' I was calling someone called Betsy. I needed to talk to her. To let her know something. So I kept speaking her name. 'Betsy.'

ELIZABETH *reels, she sits down.*

ELIZABETH. What did you need to let her know?

TERENCE. I don't know, I can't remember. All I know is that there was this thing I felt – like an urge, I suppose, a powerful, persistent urge to speak to Betsy.

VANESSA. Who's Betsy?

ELIZABETH. I am.

VANESSA. Darling, you're Elizabeth, not Betsy. I mean it may be a common diminutive but I've known you for over thirty years and nobody has ever called you Betsy.

ELIZABETH. Only Edgar.

Pause.

Our secret names for each other. I was Betsy, he was Bob. It was a private thing, like a little game. The names we used for each other when we were alone. Nobody else knew them. Not even Harold.

HAROLD. Apart from his friend Terence of course. Boys share secrets. I think we should go to bed now. In the morning, in the clear light of day perhaps you can explain to us what all this is about, young man.

TERENCE. Explain?

HAROLD. What exactly it is you're playing at I mean.

TERENCE. I'm not playing at anything, sir.

HAROLD. Why it is that you've decided to play this cruel game on my wife.

ELIZABETH. Harold.

TERENCE. I assure you, sir, I am not playing any sort of game at all. I am not some kind of sadist.

VANESSA. Terence can't hurt a soul.

HAROLD. Well then, I'm sure there's another rational explanation. I look forward to hearing it in the morning otherwise you can pack your bags and be on your way.

GEOFFREY. Steady on, Harold.

TERENCE. Fry us an egg, Betsy.

ELIZABETH*'s hand comes to her mouth and she gasps in shock.*

VANESSA. Darling, what are you talking about?

GEOFFREY. Fry you *an egg*?

TERENCE. Yes, I think so. That's what he's saying. He keeps saying it, over and over. An egg. That's what he says.

HAROLD. That's what who says?

TERENCE. He's saying it now. Over and over again. He keeps saying it. In my head, in my head.

VANESSA. My dear boy, you're scaring me.

GEOFFREY. Are you feeling all right, old chap?

TERENCE. Fry us an egg. Fry us an egg. Fry us an egg, Betsy.

TERENCE *suddenly falls to the ground and begins convulsing on the floor.* VANESSA *lets out a small scream and, with* GEOFFREY, *runs up to him and tries to grab hold of him. After shaking violently for a few seconds, he loses consciousness.*

VANESSA. Oh my dear God, what's wrong with him?

GEOFFREY. He's gone stone cold.

VANESSA. Terence my darling, my darling boy, wake up.

GEOFFREY. His whole body was shaking like a leaf.

HAROLD. Has this happened before?

GEOFFREY. No, never, never.

VANESSA. Terence my love, can you hear me?

HAROLD. The boy's obviously an epileptic.

GEOFFREY. Rubbish, I tell you nothing like this has ever happened before.

HAROLD. Maybe he's play-acting or something.

VANESSA. Why on earth would he do that?

HAROLD. You'd have to ask him.

GEOFFREY. Now look here, Harold, I understand this is all very upsetting but there's nothing to be gained by accusing my son of these outrageous –

EILEEN *runs in.*

EILEEN. Oh Good Lord, sir, ma'am, what's been happening? I heard the scream and thought you were all being murdered in your beds and then I heard you all running downstairs and I've been hiding because I fancied there were intruders in the house and –

HAROLD. Nobody's been murdered and there are no intruders or ghosts or goblins, Eileen. Mr Avery has fallen ill that's all.

GEOFFREY. I think we ought to call a doctor.

VANESSA. Yes, Harold, please.

HAROLD. Eileen, I'd like you to call Dr Gibbons and tell him to come here as soon as he can. And on your way back bring a glass of cold water and a blanket.

EILEEN. Yes, sir.

She goes.

HAROLD (*indicating the sofa*). Let's sit him up here.

GEOFFREY. That's a good idea.

HAROLD. Grab him by the legs, Geoffrey, I'll get the arms.

VANESSA. Be careful.

They pick him up carefully and rest him on the sofa.

Put the cushion under his head.

GEOFFREY *does this*.

GEOFFREY. There. That's better.

Pause.

VANESSA. I've never had such a fright in my life.

GEOFFREY. The way he shook.

VANESSA. Salivating at the mouth like a rabid dog.

HAROLD. You say this has never happened before?

GEOFFREY. And what was he saying before it all happened?
Something about a voice telling him to say it. Something
about an egg.

VANESSA. 'Fry us an egg, Betsy' is what he said. He kept
saying it again and again… 'Fry us an egg, fry us an egg.'

GEOFFREY. How very peculiar.

VANESSA. Oh, my poor boy.

Pause.

ELIZABETH. It's what he used to say to me. Edgar.

Pause.

Mocking me. Because he always used to say I couldn't. 'You
wouldn't know your way around a kitchen,' he used to say.
'Wouldn't know a grater from a whisk. What would happen
if your servants all went on strike?' he'd ask. 'You'd starve.'
And then, when we were alone and he wanted to tease me
he'd say, 'Fry us an egg, Betsy. Go on, prove that you can do
it. Fry us an egg.' It always made me laugh.

HAROLD. I've never heard that.

ELIZABETH. Because we never shared it. There was a whole territory that wasn't yours, Harold. There are things that happen and are said between mothers and children and no one else.

VANESSA. But Terence must have known.

ELIZABETH. Must he?

HAROLD. Of course he must.

ELIZABETH. Why are you so sure of that?

HAROLD. Because, Elizabeth, I am not willing to entertain ludicrous notions of the supernatural. I will not stand here in my own house and allow you or anyone else for that matter to talk such mindless drivel.

VANESSA (*to* ELIZABETH). Perhaps, my darling, there's another explanation for it.

HAROLD. I'm almost certain that there is. I'm sure your Dr Freud and some of his Viennese colleagues would have quite a lot to say about what has driven your – about what has driven young Terence here – to behave in such a confounding way tonight. Perhaps our own Dr Gibbons, though not possessing as sophisticated a grasp on the subject of human psychology will nevertheless provide his own theory as to what has caused this evening's events. But I will not hear of the other stuff.

ELIZABETH. 'The other stuff.'

HAROLD. I'm sorry, Elizabeth, but we need to keep our heads about us.

EILEEN *returns with a glass of water and a blanket.*

EILEEN. Dr Gibbons said he'll be here in five minutes, sir, as long as he can get the motor started. It's been giving him problems lately, he said, especially in the cold.

GEOFFREY. Thank you, Eileen, why don't you give me that?

She gives him the blanket and he throws it over TERENCE.

VANESSA *takes the water from her.*

VANESSA. Darling, try and have a sip of water.

HAROLD. Maybe you should throw it in his face. That should bring him to his senses.

VANESSA. That's a good boy, just sip it gently.

TERENCE *begins to sip the water but then suddenly chokes on it a little. He sputters and coughs and regains consciousness.*

TERENCE. What happened?

GEOFFREY. Welcome back to reality, boy.

TERENCE. What's happening?

VANESSA. You gave us such a terrible fright you know. Writhing and twitching on the floor like a man possessed.

TERENCE. I felt as if I was.

GEOFFREY. Well, it's all over now, thank heavens.

VANESSA. Yes. And in the morning we can go for a long walk and get some fresh air.

HAROLD. Please don't take this the wrong way, Vanessa, but I do think that the best thing for you to do in the morning is to return to London. Terence is obviously under a great deal of strain and I'm not sure that Yorkshire is doing him much good.

ELIZABETH. I want him to stay.

HAROLD. And I think they should return to London. And sometimes, Elizabeth, what I say is the law of the land I'm afraid, whether you like it or not.

ELIZABETH. What did he want to say to me, Terence?

TERENCE. I beg your pardon?

ELIZABETH. You said he needed to talk to me. He needed to let me know something. And I'm asking you again if you remember what it was?

TERENCE. I can't. I wish, but the thing is –

ELIZABETH. What was it?

TERENCE. I can't remember, I'm sorry. My head is throbbing so.

VANESSA. The doctor will be here soon, darling, he'll give you something.

TERENCE. I'm sorry, I can't remember anything. It's all a bit of a fog I'm afraid.

ELIZABETH. It's all right, I understand.

Pause.

GEOFFREY. I don't know about you, Harold, but I rather need a shot of something.

HAROLD. I'll pour you a Scotch.

He walks over to the drinks cabinet and pours two glasses of Scotch, one for GEOFFREY *and one for himself.*

GEOFFREY. Maybe whilst we're waiting for the doctor we can change the subject and talk about something a little more cheerful.

VANESSA. Yes, maybe you can tell us a few jokes, Geoffrey, or perhaps we can play a game of bridge.

GEOFFREY. Well, I just think that things being as they are –

VANESSA. Don't be ridiculous, we've just had a very traumatic experience and there's no use pretending that none of it happened.

GEOFFREY. Well, there's no use dwelling on it either.

VANESSA. Nobody's dwelling on it, Geoffrey. We're just all trying to understand it.

HAROLD *hands* GEOFFREY *his drink.*

HAROLD. I apologise, young man, if I came across rather aggressively.

GEOFFREY. I must say, you did a little.

HAROLD. But you must understand that when one is confronted in the middle of the night by somebody pretending – by somebody speaking words and names that only one's son – one's *dead* son happened to know – it is rather difficult to keep one's rag. I think it's natural.

TERENCE. Please don't apologise. I think I would have probably reacted in a very similar way. I have never experienced anything quite like this and I too am very disturbed by it.

HAROLD. And it was hasty and ill-judged of me to accuse you of malicious motives.

VANESSA. Terence isn't like that.

HAROLD. No, of course.

Pause.

So perhaps what has happened has something to do with one's – well, with Terence's – with that part of his mind that isn't fully conscious. I won't proclaim myself an expert on the subject and understand little of all that – but what I am suggesting is that maybe returning here after all these years has stirred certain parts of your mind – those parts that usually remain hidden in dark corners – into some sort of overdrive shall we say. Perhaps there are things – *emotional* things, God knows what, again this territory is one with which I am not familiar – that have unleashed this reaction. The fact that you are back in the house where you last saw my son and have had a reunion with my wife and myself, well, perhaps you have reacted to all that in this violent way because certain memories are too painful to *consciously* acknowledge.

Pause.

Does that make any sense at all?

TERENCE. Yes, it does, it does.

GEOFFREY. Do you know, Harold, you're beginning to sound rather like that Dr Freud yourself, I'm impressed.

TERENCE. Carry on, Mr Pritchard. You haven't finished have you?

HAROLD. Well, what I'm suggesting is that you did in fact know these things as a boy – you knew for instance that Edgar's name for his mother was Betsy and he had mentioned to you how he used to tease her by saying 'fry us an egg, Betsy' and all that but that you've simply forgotten it. But that that part of your mind that I was talking about hadn't forgotten either of those things at all.

TERENCE. Yes, yes.

HAROLD. And all that's happened is that these memories have now released themselves from that dark corner and have forced you into speaking them – albeit in a strange and disconcerting way.

ELIZABETH. Why can't you just accept that there are things you will never fully understand, Harold? Does that make you feel powerless?

The doorbell rings.

EILEEN. Oh, that'll be the doctor, sir.

HAROLD. Well, don't just stand there, go and open the door.

EILEEN. Yes, sir.

She goes.

TERENCE. I must say I rather agree with Mr Pritchard's analysis. And come to think of it I was apprehensive about returning here even though many years had passed. I've often thought about how terrible it was that poor Edgar died the day after we'd all left and also about the last few days we were here and how close the two of us were. And there's no question that he may well have mentioned those things to me in passing. So yes, I think I rather agree with you, Mr Pritchard.

HAROLD. I believe that's the most reasonable explanation for all this.

ELIZABETH. Reasonable, yes.

EILEEN *returns, followed by* DR GIBBONS, *who is carrying a bag and looks as if he has been battling the elements.*

EILEEN. Dr Gibbons, sir.

DR GIBBONS. That raging wind nearly blew my motor into a ditch. Mr Pritchard, sir, Mrs Pritchard.

HAROLD. Thank you for coming so swiftly, doctor, though it may have been in vain, young Terence here is looking a whole lot perkier than he was a few minutes ago.

TERENCE. Even more cause for embarrassment.

DR GIBBONS. What seems to be the problem?

VANESSA. Hello, doctor, I'm Vanessa Avery.

DR GIBBONS. How d'you do, Mrs Avery?

VANESSA. I've been better. My son here had some sort of fit a few minutes ago, he went into convulsions and was shaking on the floor in the most appalling way.

DR GIBBONS. Is there a history of any sort of –

GEOFFREY. No, nothing at all, no history of anything untoward, he's always been as fit as a fiddle.

DR GIBBONS. And how did it all start then?

TERENCE. Doctor, I really do feel rather ashamed to have got you out of bed in the middle of the night like this. I'm absolutely fine, I think I just had something of an – let's see, how can I describe it – I think, loath as I am to admit it – that it was something of an emotional nature.

DR GIBBONS. Your mother said you had convulsions.

TERENCE. I did, yes, but I think that what brought it on was…

DR GIBBONS. Was what?

TERENCE. I think, if truth be told, that I just need a good rest, that's all.

DR GIBBONS. I'll still need to examine you, young man.

TERENCE. Yes, I do understand. Shall we…

DR GIBBONS. We'll need some privacy and you can tell me in your own words exactly what happened tonight.

HAROLD. Good idea. Why don't the two of you go upstairs and then afterwards you can come down, doctor, and tell us what you think.

DR GIBBONS. Yes, sir.

TERENCE (*slowly standing*). Thank you all for being so understanding and I apologise once again for the histrionics I forced you to watch.

VANESSA. No need to apologise, my darling, you haven't done a thing wrong.

TERENCE. I shall see you all in the morning.

He walks up to HAROLD.

And thank you, sir, for your thoughts on it. Do you know, I think they're rather accurate. It's quite ironic thinking of all the conversations we've been having since we got here. It's all very well saying that we need to reintroduce the mystical into our lives but it's not very pleasant when one feels that the mystical has marked one out for some special purpose. Quite the opposite.

DR GIBBONS. Mystical?

TERENCE. Goodnight, all.

HAROLD. Goodnight, Terence.

TERENCE *begins to make his way towards the door, closely followed by* DR GIBBONS.

ELIZABETH. Do you believe, Dr Gibbons, that the dead can contact us through the living?

They both stop.

HAROLD. For God's sake, Elizabeth, please.

VANESSA. Darling, I really think you ought to get to bed.

TERENCE. Yes.

DR GIBBONS. I'll be up in a minute, Mr Avery.

TERENCE. Of course. Thank you, doctor.

TERENCE *leaves the room.*

DR GIBBONS. That's an interesting question, Mrs Pritchard.

HAROLD. It's a ridiculous question, doctor, and I'm only sorry you've been asked it. You have to forgive my wife, the evening's events have unsettled her.

ELIZABETH. Do you, doctor?

Pause. He thinks about how to best respond.

DR GIBBONS. Well, I'm a man of science. So sceptical too.

Pause.

Any talk of the supernatural – of the metaphysical side of
life has me usually rushing for the nearest door. It makes me
uncomfortable. Not because it frightens me – no, far from it.
Only because the subject seems to attract a somewhat – how
shall I put it – slow-witted pool of admirers. Oh, please don't
misunderstand me I'm not –

ELIZABETH. Don't worry, doctor, I won't take the remark
personally.

DR GIBBONS. Heaven forbid. And perhaps slow-witted is the
wrong word in this instance in any case. The less educated
shall we say. Superstition and ignorance often go hand in
hand.

HAROLD. My thoughts exactly.

DR GIBBONS. But that doesn't exclude things from happening
from time to time, Mrs Pritchard, which completely
confound our rational selves and for which we can find no
discernible answers.

GEOFFREY. So true.

DR GIBBONS. A particular incident comes to mind. It
happened a few years ago in one of the mining villages near
Peterborough. The miners and their families – well, perhaps
this has something to do with what I was just saying about a
lack of education – but the miners and their families are
often prone to believing things that the rest of us would be
quick to dismiss as fantastical.

ELIZABETH. Maybe it's simply to do with the fact that their
experience of life is so different to ours.

DR GIBBONS. They have a woman in one of the villages –
'the layer-on of hands' they call her and all I can say is she's
good competition. It's not an exaggeration to say that with
many ailments they rush to her for remedy long before they

come knocking on my own door. The woman, they say, has hands that heal.

HAROLD. Hands that heal, eh?

DR GIBBONS. Well, a few years back this same woman who is also said by the miners and their families – some of them mind you, not all – to have some sort of what you would call *psychic* abilities was called to the house of one of the miners in which there'd been some sort of disturbance. There were six people living in the small house – the miner and his wife and their four children. Apparently objects had been seen flying around the house –

HAROLD. Insanity.

DR GIBBONS. – a frying pan or whatnot would suddenly fling itself across the kitchen say. I never witnessed this myself but spoke to a number of people who swore that they had. And then there was a persistent smell of rotting meat. But even though they searched everywhere to find the source of the stench, going so far as to pull up the floorboards to look for it, they never found a thing. And then this woman – the 'layer-on of hands' – spent a week in the house, sleeping on the kitchen floor and all of a sudden on the seventh day, she seemed to be taken over by some sort of – well, let me word it a different way – she began behaving very oddly, speaking in a voice which wasn't her own but belonged to a young girl and also making all sorts of terrible groaning noises as if she was in the most appalling pain. Eventually she started repeating the same words over and over again and it transpired to be an address three streets away. She kept repeating something along the lines of 'the third house down on Chapel Way'. Well, finally a number of people took the initiative to make their way to the house she kept describing. It was an old derelict place, unlived-in for some time. And in there – down in the small, dank cellar – they found the skeleton of a young woman who had been brutally murdered and dismembered.

VANESSA. How ghastly.

DR GIBBONS. And then – and this is the part that makes my skin crawl – they came to discover that the man who had murdered this poor woman was none other than the miner in whose house the strange happenings had first occurred.

HAROLD. A haunting tale, Dr Gibbons. But I must say I'm surprised by the fact that you entertain the possibility of it being anything other than fiction.

DR GIBBONS. Like you, Mr Pritchard, I'm sure, I am alarmed and made uncomfortable by the possibility that there are things I may never fully grasp or comprehend.

HAROLD. And there is a slight problem that I have with your story, doctor. Well, not so much a problem as a query.

DR GIBBONS. What is it?

HAROLD. Why did the miner let this 'layer-on of hands' into his house? Why did he allow her into his home if he believed it would be likely to lead to the discovery of his crime?

DR GIBBONS. A good question, Mr Pritchard. Perhaps he was just exhausted of carrying the guilt.

There's a loud clap of thunder and suddenly the electrics are affected – the lights momentarily fail and the room is plunged into darkness.

GEOFFREY. Good heavens.

VANESSA. What on earth…

HAROLD. That's all we bloody need.

Then, they suddenly switch on again. And, as if out of nowhere, TERENCE *has appeared at the bottom of the stairs. He is only half-dressed, his top half is bare, though he is still wearing his pyjama bottoms. He has a strange expression on his face, not quite his own.*

ELIZABETH. Terence.

VANESSA lets out a yelp of surprise.

VANESSA. Dear God, darling, you gave me the fright of my life.

GEOFFREY. Why aren't you wearing your top, Terence?

VANESSA. Darling, you're only half-dressed. And what are you doing here anyway? The doctor is coming up to you now, he was just talking to us.

GEOFFREY. You'll catch a chill, my boy.

DR GIBBONS. I was just on my way, young man.

VANESSA. You gave me a terrible fright, just standing there.

GEOFFREY. Get back to bed, Terence, there's a good chap.

VANESSA. Did you hear what I said? You really shouldn't be down here, not after what you've been through. Darling?

TERENCE *does not answer. Slowly, as if in a trance, he walks up to* HAROLD. *When he speaks his voice has changed, he sounds like a young boy.*

TERENCE. Thank you for the chocolates, Father.

HAROLD. I'm not your father so don't call me it.

TERENCE. It's very kind of you. And you know they're my favourite.

HAROLD. Stop it. Do you hear what I'm saying to you? Stop it now, otherwise I've a good mind to beat you to a hair's width of your life.

VANESSA. Harold, please!

TERENCE. Mother, Father's bought me chocolates.

ELIZABETH. I know he has, my angel. From Leeds.

TERENCE. I know, Mother. He must have bought them yesterday.

ELIZABETH. He did, my darling, he did. Because he drove the Averys to Leeds so that they could get their train back to London and then he had a business meeting too and he stopped off at the arcade after that and bought you those chocolates, the ones you like so much.

TERENCE. Thank you, Father.

HAROLD. Stop it!

VANESSA. Stop it, Terence, stop calling him 'Father', stop speaking in that voice, you're frightening me.

ELIZABETH. How could he know, Harold? How could he know these things?

GEOFFREY. Know what?

ELIZABETH. How could he know that on the morning he went missing, that very morning, his father gave him a box of chocolates that he'd bought him in Leeds the day before…

TERENCE. Thank you, Father.

ELIZABETH. How could he know?

HAROLD. This is madness, sheer madness I tell you.

DR GIBBONS. I've never seen the like.

ELIZABETH. How?

TERENCE *walks up to* ELIZABETH *and mimes handing her something.*

TERENCE. And here's heather for you, Mother, because you love it so.

ELIZABETH. And that afterwards he went and gathered heather for me and gave me it tied in a little string? Just before, just before he left, it was the last thing he did.

TERENCE. Because you love it so.

ELIZABETH. I've never told a living soul, how could he know?

TERENCE. And now, Mother, there's something I need to tell you.

ELIZABETH. What is it, my love? What is it? What is it?

HAROLD. Stop this madness! Stop it now.

VANESSA. Terence, I beg you.

ELIZABETH. What is it?

TERENCE. Mother, Father, you must take me to Bracken Moor. I have to tell you what it was like. I have to tell you what happened in the dark. What happened at Bracken Moor.

EILEEN *lets out a spine-chilling scream and falls to her knees.*

Blackout.

End of Act One.

*As at the beginning of the play, the actors who are on stage at
the top of the act – in this instance those playing the parts of*
JOHN *and* EILEEN *– walk on while the house lights are still
on. The actor playing* JOHN *puts on his coat while the actor
playing* EILEEN *brings on a tray of tea things and rests it on a
table. She rearranges her costume a little and gets into her
position for the top of the act.*

Blackout.

ACT TWO

Scene One

Lights up.

*The following afternoon. It continues to be stormy though the
wind has abated a little. The windows, however, are being
pelted with rain.*

EILEEN *is standing in the middle of the room and preparing
for tea. She has a tray of cups and saucers and is carefully
placing them one by one onto the coffee table. But as she sees to
the task her hands are slightly shaking.*

JOHN *is there in his coat, which is soaking wet.*

EILEEN. So you understand, Mr Bailey, this is not the time for
any sort of business.

JOHN. I can see that now.

EILEEN. Perhaps it were best for you to return in the morning,
sir.

JOHN. Yes.

EILEEN. Because I can not imagine that after all that's happened – oh, the horrible, horrible things, Mr Bailey, which I saw with my own two eyes – well, I don't imagine that after all that poor Mr Pritchard would have the head for any sort of business.

JOHN. I expect not.

EILEEN. He turned as white as the whitest sheet when we were there and poor Mrs Pritchard wailing like some sort of – well, like an animal, Mr Bailey, if you'll forgive me for saying, like a trapped deer or something and the boy – that strange, haunted Mr Avery, rolling on the floor down in the pit, his clothes covered in mud and his hair matted with it. They'd thrown down a rope ladder you see and they wanted me there so that I could help carry things and we all went down into the pit where the poor boy breathed his last all those years ago and it was as if we were descending into the bowels of the earth, as if we were entering Hell itself.

JOHN. That can't have been pleasant.

EILEEN. Oh, it wasn't, Mr Bailey, it wasn't, it wasn't and – (*Suddenly drops the cup and saucer she is holding and bursts into tears.*) and I don't know what to do with myself, Mr Bailey, I don't know what to do but I can't stay in this house any more even though I'd feel terrible for leaving them, especially poor Mrs Pritchard who's like a ghost herself, wandering the corridors like a sleepwalker these last ten years, but I can't stay, Mr Bailey, even though I have nowhere else to go and my mother and brothers to support but I can't stay, not after the things I've seen and heard and I haven't slept in three days and I think I'm losing my mind, I'm ever so frightened, Mr Bailey, ever so unhappy, but what can I do.

JOHN. But did the boy say anything?

EILEEN (*trying to pull herself together*). Oh, I do beg your pardon, sir, for making such a fuss and crying and all but I really am ever so unhappy.

JOHN. Of course you are.

Pause.

EILEEN. No, the boy didn't say a word, Mr Bailey, just rolled
on the floor making these noises as if he were in the most
terrible anguish and tearing his clothes off as if he was trying
to escape his very own body, it makes me shiver just
remembering it.

Pause.

So they've covered him in a blanket and are carrying him
home now with Mrs Pritchard walking in their wake asking
him all the time, 'What is that you need me to know, Edgar,
what is it that you need me to know?' but the boy not saying
a word just rolling his head around like someone who's lost
their mind for good. But they sent me ahead so that I could
light the fire and make some tea for them, God knows they'll
need it after hours in that cold, damp place.

JOHN. What a terrible situation.

EILEEN. Oh, it is, Mr Bailey, it is. And it makes you think
about all sorts of things.

JOHN. What sort of things, Miss Hannaway?

EILEEN. I mean about your own life, Mr Bailey, and about
what it means to be a human being.

JOHN. How do you mean?

EILEEN. About what all the pain is about and the loss and the
cruel things we do to each other and if there's any meaning
to it at all or if we were just put on this earth to suffer and
die. Oh Jesus, forgive me for even thinking this way.

JOHN. Miss Hannaway –

EILEEN. Oh, I'm sorry, Mr Bailey, I'm not making any sense at
all.

JOHN. On the contrary, Miss Hannaway, I think you're making
a whole lot of sense. It's a shame though that it takes such
frightful things to happen before we question things the way
we ought.

EILEEN (*crossing herself*). I'll be going to church in the
morning and doing a whole lot of praying, that's for certain.

JOHN. Whatever brings you comfort, Miss Hannaway.

EILEEN. Oh God help us all, Mr Bailey, God help us all.

There is the sound of a door opening and voices entering the house.

Oh, there they are now.

JOHN. I'd better be on my way then.

EILEEN. And I need to get the pot of tea. Why don't you follow me, sir, and I'll let you out the back way.

JOHN. Thank you, Miss Hannaway.

EILEEN. And maybe you can come back at a better time.

JOHN. I shall.

EILEEN leads JOHN out of the room.

For a few seconds the room is empty. Then the door to the hallway opens and they all enter: HAROLD and GEOFFREY, half-carrying TERENCE who is semi-conscious, and behind them ELIZABETH and VANESSA. The men carry TERENCE over to the sofa and lay him down on it. All of them are covered in mud and dirt, but especially TERENCE who is in a state of semi-dress, with a blanket thrown over him but with no shoes or socks on his feet.

GEOFFREY. That'll do.

VANESSA. I really think we should take him upstairs instead, Geoffrey.

ELIZABETH. He can rest here for a little while.

VANESSA. And he'll need a wash, we need to wash him.

HAROLD. We all will, look at us, covered in grime and dirt, as if we've carried that damned place with us.

GEOFFREY. Those bloody rats.

ELIZABETH. Why don't you go upstairs and rest a little, I'll stay here with Terence and if he wakes in the meantime I'll be sure to call you.

GEOFFREY. And we can have a wash ourselves and get into a clean set of clothes.

VANESSA. I just don't think it's a good idea, I want him to come upstairs with us.

ELIZABETH. It's warm here, he'll be comfortable. Why don't you go and rest, I'll stay by his side.

VANESSA. I said I don't think it's a good idea.

ELIZABETH. You could even start pouring him a bath and Harold will help him up in no time.

VANESSA. My dear, you're not listening, I said I don't think it's a good idea.

ELIZABETH. Why ever not?

VANESSA. Because I don't, I don't, I DON'T!

Pause.

I'm sorry, Elizabeth, but I don't, I just don't like it at all, not one bit, all this that's been happening.

HAROLD. None of this is Elizabeth's doing, Vanessa.

VANESSA. And I'm sorry to have to say this –

GEOFFREY. Careful, darling.

VANESSA. But it's as if you want something from him.

ELIZABETH. Want something?

VANESSA. Yes, it's as if you do and I can't lie, I don't like it one bit. And I don't think we should have taken him there, to that horrible place, and I bitterly regret we did and that we had to witness what we did and I think that Harold's right and the best thing for us to do is to get on the next train out of here and head straight back to London.

ELIZABETH. He was the one who wanted us to go.

VANESSA. So I'd rather appreciate it, Harold, if you asked your man to drive us into Leeds in the next hour so that we can get on the train and leave you all in peace.

ELIZABETH. In peace, yes.

HAROLD. You won't make the evening train, you might as well leave in the morning.

VANESSA. Well then we can stay at an hotel or something.

GEOFFREY. Darling.

VANESSA. Because I really can't bear this any longer.

HAROLD. None of us can, Vanessa.

TERENCE *makes a noise, as if he is in discomfort and shivers quite violently.*

VANESSA. He's cold, we need to put his sweater on again, I don't know why you took it off to begin with. Geoffrey, where have you put it?

ELIZABETH. He pulled it off himself as we made our way back and fought when I tried to put it on him again.

HAROLD (*handing* VANESSA *the sweater*). Here we are.

VANESSA. And his socks too, for Heaven's sake.

HAROLD. And the socks.

ELIZABETH *takes* TERENCE's *socks from* HAROLD.

ELIZABETH. Those too, he pulled them off himself.

VANESSA. That's neither here nor there, Elizabeth, it was freezing cold and he didn't know what it was he was doing, he'll catch his death.

ELIZABETH *kneels down and starts to put his socks on.*

ELIZABETH. I'll put his socks on and he'll be warm again and you can go upstairs and pour him a bath and in less than ten minutes we'll be up and he'll be well once more, you'll see, Vanessa, your boy will be well again.

VANESSA. Geoffrey.

GEOFFREY. Yes, dear. Harold, I really think we need to draw a line here. The best thing to do is to let the boy come up with us.

HAROLD. Elizabeth.

ELIZABETH. He said he needs to speak to me. Five minutes that's all.

VANESSA *tries to move* ELIZABETH *out of the way as she starts putting the socks on* TERENCE*'s feet.*

VANESSA. Leave that, Elizabeth, I shall do it, it's fine.

ELIZABETH. It's all right, I'm nearly finished, let me.

VANESSA. I said please leave it, Elizabeth.

ELIZABETH. We need to be left alone for just a moment. Maybe that's why he hasn't spoken. He said he had something to tell me.

VANESSA. He may have said many things, Elizabeth, but the time has come to put an end to all of it.

ELIZABETH. He said he had something to say to his mother.

VANESSA. I am his mother, Elizabeth, *I am* his mother.

ELIZABETH. So let us be for just one minute, I beg you.

VANESSA *becomes more forceful in moving* ELIZABETH *out of the way.*

VANESSA. Leave him alone please, Elizabeth, put those down and leave him alone.

ELIZABETH. One minute is all I'm asking for.

VANESSA. And I'm sorry you lost your boy, Elizabeth, God only knows how sorry I am, but I'm not prepared to lose mine as well.

ELIZABETH. How do you mean?

VANESSA. To this madness that's gripped him since we got here. YOURS IS LOST ALREADY, MINE I WILL HOLD ON TO WITH ALL MY STRENGTH AND MIGHT!

She bursts into tears.

I'm so sorry, what a cruel, cruel thing to say.

ELIZABETH. It's all right, Vanessa, it's all right.

VANESSA. What a monstrous thing to say.

ELIZABETH. Really, it's all right. You're upset.

VANESSA. I'm so sorry, I'm so sorry, I'm so sorry.

ELIZABETH. Stay for the night and go tomorrow, I beg you.

VANESSA. I'm not sure it's for the best.

ELIZABETH. And in the morning we'll put everything behind us.

HAROLD. I asked the girl to make some tea. Why don't you go and change and then come downstairs and have a cup. We'll look after him, don't worry yourselves.

GEOFFREY. Good idea. A cup of tea smacks of a little sanity.

VANESSA. All right then.

VANESSA *walks up to* ELIZABETH *and kisses her.*

I'm sorry, my dear. My nerves.

ELIZABETH. You needn't apologise, Vanessa, I understand.

GEOFFREY. Come on, my girl.

VANESSA. Ten minutes, Elizabeth. And then upstairs.

ELIZABETH. Ten minutes, no longer.

VANESSA *and* GEOFFREY *leave.*

ELIZABETH *and* HAROLD *are left alone with* TERENCE. *Neither of them speak for some time.* ELIZABETH *sits on the floor by* TERENCE*'s side and picks up one of his hands.*

His nails are covered in dirt.

HAROLD. They would be, wouldn't they? The way he was scratching and clawing the earth.

EILEEN *comes in with the pot of tea.*

EILEEN. The tea's ready, ma'am.

ELIZABETH. Thank you, Eileen, put it there on the table.

EILEEN. Yes, ma'am.

ELIZABETH. And then I want you to bring me something.

EILEEN. What is it, ma'am?

ELIZABETH. Pour some of the boiling water from the kettle into a bowl and bring it to me with a bar of soap and a washrag.

EILEEN. Yes, ma'am.

She goes. HAROLD *goes over to the tea.*

HAROLD. Shall I pour you a cup?

ELIZABETH. In a little while.

He pours himself a cup and goes to stand by the window, looking out at the rain. ELIZABETH *remains by* TERENCE*'s side.*

He looks more peaceful now. His breathing has quietened, and his pulse is a little slower.

HAROLD. That's a good thing.

ELIZABETH. It is, yes.

Pause.

Do you remember about three weeks before the… three weeks before we lost him, we spent that Sunday over towards Sheffield and had a picnic on that hillside.

HAROLD. I think so, yes.

ELIZABETH. It was a glorious day. And fun too. He sat on your knees in the motor and pretended he was driving it.

HAROLD. I remember. It was a pleasant Sunday.

ELIZABETH. But then your mood changed.

HAROLD. Did it?

ELIZABETH. He said something. Edgar did. And you disapproved.

HAROLD. I don't remember.

ELIZABETH. You said it was a girly thing to say and then you were in the foulest mood all afternoon.

HAROLD. I really don't remember.

ELIZABETH. But it wounded him and I remember noticing that his eyes were moist with tears around the edges. But of course he held back because if he had cried you would have become even angrier.

HAROLD. I was trying to instil in him some understanding of what the world expects of a man.

ELIZABETH. Is that what you were doing?

Pause.

I can't remember what it was he said. Something silly, innocuous, the way children talk. But you punished him for it.

HAROLD. I really don't recall it.

EILEEN *returns with a bowl of steaming water, a bar of soap and a washrag.*

EILEEN. Here you are, ma'am.

ELIZABETH. Thank you, Eileen, you can leave it here.

EILEEN *places the bowl, the soap and the washrag by* ELIZABETH*'s side.*

That'll be all, thank you, Eileen.

EILEEN. Yes, ma'am.

She goes. ELIZABETH *begins to soak the washrag in the steaming water.*

ELIZABETH. I always felt, Harold, that what you wanted most from Edgar was for him to reflect something of yourself.

HAROLD. Why are you saying these things now?

ELIZABETH. Because I never have before.

Pause.

As if you wanted him to be an extension of yourself, not a person in his own right.

HAROLD. He was a child, Elizabeth.

ELIZABETH. And I wonder if we're all extensions. If you've ever really known how to see people for what they are.

Pause.

Harold, can you leave me alone with him for a minute? I want to… Could you? Not longer than a minute. I just want to wash the dirt from under his nails but I want to do it alone.

HAROLD. I shall be in my study. If he stirs, call me.

ELIZABETH. I shall, thank you.

HAROLD *leaves the room and goes to his study.*

ELIZABETH *picks up the washrag, squeezes it and begins to clean the areas around* TERENCE's *nails. A few seconds pass like this and then, quietly, she begins to speak to him.*

I need to talk to you. I don't know if you can hear me or if you can understand me but there's something that I need to tell you.

Pause.

I love you. I love you with all my heart and my soul and from the very depth of my being.

I was so grateful because when I knew you I learnt the meaning of faith. How could I not believe in a good future when I held you in my arms and cradled you? How could I not believe that there was a beautiful plan of which we were both a part and which would lead us to some beckoning place where God's face would finally be revealed? So thank you for those years of faith, my angel.

Pause. She places the washrag into the bowl of water and picks up the boy's head in her hands and cradles him.

I ran, my love, and screamed and shouted and ran and ran and ran. Even in the night and all hours of the day, through the fields and the backs of houses, in the villages and on the hills and by the river too and as I ran all I kept doing was shouting your name. And I'm still running, and I'll be running till the day I die. But I'm sorry I didn't find you in time.

Suddenly, TERENCE *starts convulsing and gasping for air and his eyes open and are full of terror.* ELIZABETH *jumps back and lets out a small scream.*

Harold! Harold, come!

As TERENCE *writhes in terror on the floor,* HAROLD *runs back into the room.*

TERENCE. Rats, Mother, rats, rats in the dark, rats, rats, rats.

ELIZABETH. Where, darling, where?

TERENCE. Rats in the dark, Mother, here in the dark, scurrying to and fro over my legs, Mother, scurry, scurry, scurry.

ELIZABETH. I'm here, darling, here, I'm here.

TERENCE. On my own, Mother, Father, on my own in the dark and I can't move my legs and the rats are running over them.

ELIZABETH. Can you hear me, my love, we're looking for you, we're looking everywhere trying to find you.

TERENCE. Pain, pain, pain, pain in my legs, running through my spine, so much pain, so much pain.

ELIZABETH. I know, my love, I know.

TERENCE. You'll find me, you'll find me, I hope you'll find me, I pray you'll find me.

ELIZABETH. Oh, my angel, my sweet angel.

TERENCE. Though I walk through the valley of the shadow of death, I will fear no evil; for Thou art with me; Thy rod and Thy staff they comfort me.

HAROLD. He prays.

TERENCE. The Lord is my shepherd, the Lord is my shepherd, the Lord is my shepherd.

ELIZABETH. Yes, my darling, yes my darling.

TERENCE. Though I walk through the valley of the shadow of death, I will fear no evil; for Thou art with me; Thy rod and Thy staff they comfort me.

ELIZABETH. Oh, my child, my poor, poor child.

TERENCE. I pray, Mother, I pray, just like you taught me, just like we did at school, I pray, Mother, pray, I pray for the pain in my legs to go away and for the rats to go, I pray, I pray, I pray. I pray for you to come and find me and I pray to remind myself of who I am.

ELIZABETH. You're a boy, *my* boy, the most beautiful boy with a soul as big as everything in the world and as infinite.

TERENCE. Where are you, Father, why aren't you here, where are you, Father?

ELIZABETH. Talk to him, Harold, speak to him.

TERENCE. Frightened, Father, frightened, frightened that you'll never find me.

ELIZABETH. We're looking for you, angel, looking everywhere.

TERENCE. Frightened that I'm all alone.

ELIZABETH. Harold, speak to him, I beg you, comfort him.

TERENCE. Mother, Father, I don't want to die.

ELIZABETH. Oh, my darling, we're looking for you, searching everywhere, calling you.

TERENCE. I am alone, I am alone, I am alone. Alone in the dark, forever alone.

ELIZABETH. No, my darling, no.

TERENCE. My God, my God, why hast Thou forsaken me?

ELIZABETH. Oh, my boy, my sweet boy.

TERENCE. Matter wins, matter, matter, matter.

ELIZABETH. No, my angel, no.

TERENCE. Death is coming, fear, fear, fear, death death, death.

ELIZABETH. I'm with you, my angel, I am with you, always with you.

TERENCE. Always alone, forever alone, in the darkness and the fear and the death forever.

ELIZABETH. No. No. No.

TERENCE collapses onto the floor and ELIZABETH *falls on him, wraps her arms around him and sobs. For a few seconds they remain like this on the ground, with* HAROLD *standing nearby looking down at them. Then, slowly,* TERENCE *stands up. He walks over to another corner of the room and kneels down again.*

TERENCE. Mother, come here, give me your hand.

She goes to him and kneels beside him. He looks into her eyes and speaks softly, simply.

This is what I needed to tell you.

ELIZABETH. What is it, my angel?

TERENCE. I know that you ran and still run, Mother. But you need to stop now.

Pause.

I know that you called my name and that you still call it. But you need to stop.

ELIZABETH. No.

And then, almost as if the words are not his own but passing through him:

TERENCE. Death is birth Mother through the flesh into the eternal life through the darkest hour back into the light I am through now Mother I am the new blades of grass in the churchyard where you buried me and the same bird that returns to the steeple every morning and the ants that walk in the cracks outside your window Mother Mother I can see you through the window and I am the boy that picks the apples from the tree at the bottom of the garden Father Mother I am the owl of the night and the cockerel that announces the morning from the farm beneath our house and Father Father I am the miners working in the dark working working working toiling toiling toiling toiling for the common good...

ELIZABETH. The common good.

TERENCE. And I am the daughters of the miners and I shall be their daughters too and their sons as well look after me Father look after me the walls are gone for ever and all is understood I am life Mother Father I am life forever here forever returning look after me Mother look after me Father we are One.

He closes his eyes and loses consciousness again.

ELIZABETH *lets out a noise, something like a wail, a guttural sound of release, as if she is letting go of something she has held onto for many years.*

Blackout.

Scene Two

The following morning. It is a sunny day outside and thick shafts of light flood into the room, brightening everything.

HAROLD *is reading the newspaper.*

EILEEN *enters. She is carrying a tray with a coffee pot and cups on it.*

EILEEN. Would you like your coffee in here, sir?

HAROLD. Yes, thank you, Eileen.

She places the tray on the coffee table and pours him a cup.

EILEEN. Cook is asking if you'd like your breakfast now, sir?

HAROLD. I won't be wanting any today, Eileen. But you best ask the Averys if they should like theirs.

EILEEN. They've already eaten breakfast, sir, they were up at the crack of dawn.

HAROLD. Did you tell Mr McLean to get the motor ready?

EILEEN. I did, sir, and I told him that Mr and Mrs Avery and young Mr Avery need to be at the train station by midday so he suggested leaving just after ten o'clock.

HAROLD. Can you notify them?

EILEEN. Oh, I have done already, sir, though young Mr Avery is still asleep. But his mother said she would wake him shortly and help him pack his bag.

HAROLD. Good.

EILEEN. Is there anything else, sir?

HAROLD. Not for the time being.

EILEEN. Thank you, sir. Do ring if you need me. I shall be upstairs helping Mrs Pritchard with her packing.

Pause.

HAROLD. Helping Mrs Pritchard with her packing?

EILEEN. Yes, sir.

HAROLD. Surely you mean Mrs Avery.

EILEEN. Oh, no, sir, I mean Mrs Pritchard. She said she needed some help packing her suitcase. She told me she's going to be visiting her sister in London for a few days.

HAROLD. Is she?

EILEEN. Oh, I thought you knew, sir.

HAROLD. I didn't.

EILEEN. Isn't that wonderful news, Mr Pritchard?

He doesn't answer. EILEEN *walks over to the window and pulls back one of the curtains to let the full force of the sun in.*

It's a beautiful day, sir.

HAROLD. Yes.

EILEEN. Nice to see the sun again, isn't it, sir?

HAROLD. Indeed.

She goes. He puts the paper down for a second, lost in thought.

GEOFFREY *walks in.*

GEOFFREY. Hello, old boy.

HAROLD. Morning, Geoffrey.

GEOFFREY. What's the news?

HAROLD. It looks as if Franco has secured the North.

GEOFFREY. Vanessa's waking the boy and then we said we'd go for a stroll in the garden.

HAROLD. Excellent idea.

GEOFFREY. Make the most of it, eh?

HAROLD. Definitely.

Pause.

Help yourself to coffee.

GEOFFREY. Do you know, I think I will.

GEOFFREY *pours himself a cup and sits down.*

What to say, eh? What to say.

HAROLD. Yes.

Pause.

GEOFFREY. I would think the most important thing for all of us now is to try and return to some kind of normality.

HAROLD. Essential, yes.

GEOFFREY. Easier said than done, of course.

HAROLD. Absolutely.

GEOFFREY. But one must make one's best effort.

HAROLD. One must.

GEOFFREY. Even though the world is changed for ever.

HAROLD. Is it?

GEOFFREY. Well, what I mean is, how can you not... I mean after... the *things*. You know.

HAROLD. The things, yes.

GEOFFREY. How can you not... review... not review, what's the word, *re-evaluate* I suppose is what I mean. Re-evaluate.

HAROLD. Re-evaluate what, Geoffrey?

GEOFFREY. Well, everything really. Life, I mean. One's perceptions at least, one's views. Nothing is what one thought it was, is it? As if one's been holding on to something concrete and then finds out that it isn't concrete at all but something entirely different. Almost as if –

HAROLD. When you walk around the garden you mustn't forget to stop off by the little wall behind the elm trees. There's a wonderful view of the meadow.

GEOFFREY. Won't you join us?

HAROLD. I'm going to have to start working I'm afraid.

GEOFFREY. Of course.

HAROLD. Lots to be getting on with.

Pause.

GEOFFREY. Take me for instance. I am surrounded by beautiful objects all day long, every day. And each object has its own unique personality and its own exclusive history. But I spend so much time either valuing these objects for their monetary worth or cataloguing them that sometimes I forget to really observe them, to *appreciate* them I suppose. The force of habit, isn't that what they say. You behave in a certain way and cease to really notice things. You forget their power and beauty and innate essence. I'm probably not making much sense –

HAROLD. Not a lot, Geoffrey.

GEOFFREY. But what I think I'm saying is that sometimes these extraordinary events occur which are so beyond one's own sphere of experience, so beyond everything one's known and recognised up till that point, well, that suddenly life seems to be new and full of infinite potential. As if your eyes have been opened for the very first time to its inexhaustible possibilities. I think most of us are walking around in a sort of slumber really.

VANESSA *and* ELIZABETH *walk in*.

VANESSA. Terence has risen at last, like Lazarus from the dead. Good morning, Harold.

HAROLD. Morning, Vanessa.

VANESSA. And Elizabeth's coming down with us and we'll drop her off at Charlotte's, isn't that marvellous?

HAROLD. I heard.

ELIZABETH. I was coming to tell you.

HAROLD. Of course.

ELIZABETH. Charlotte can't quite believe it. She's emptying the little spare room for me.

VANESSA. Are you quite sure you don't want to come and stay at ours?

ELIZABETH. No, it's fine, really, but thank you, Vanessa. It'll be nice to spend some time with my sister.

GEOFFREY. Of course.

ELIZABETH. After all it's been years and years.

VANESSA. She'll be happy to see you again. Well, everybody will. I'm already making plans to show you off to all and sundry.

ELIZABETH. Oh, Vanessa, I beg you.

VANESSA. Beg me what, darling?

ELIZABETH. I just want a little time. And then we'll see.

VANESSA. Of course. Of course, I understand, trust me.

ELIZABETH. I do.

GEOFFREY. Well then you need your head examined.

VANESSA. Shut up, Geoffrey, and drink your coffee.

Pause.

Terence says he's never felt better and do you know, I don't think he's ever looked it. The colour's back in his cheeks and the sparkle's in his eyes.

GEOFFREY. That's our boy.

VANESSA. And he says he doesn't remember a thing about yesterday.

ELIZABETH. I'd imagine that's a good thing.

VANESSA. I think so too. Who'd want to remember... well, who'd want to remember all the dreadful things that happened to him.

GEOFFREY. Who indeed.

VANESSA. But he's looking a whole lot better.

Pause.

Come on then, let's get that walk in.

GEOFFREY. Round the garden, yes.

VANESSA. Don't worry, you lazy sod, no further. We shan't be climbing any mountains.

GEOFFREY. What a shame.

ELIZABETH. I'll join you in just a minute.

VANESSA. All right, my darling.

ELIZABETH. And then we'll have the suitcases brought downstairs and loaded into the motor.

VANESSA. Come on then, Geoffrey, move those ancient, sagging limbs.

VANESSA *and* GEOFFREY *leave the room. A few seconds pass before* ELIZABETH *speaks.*

ELIZABETH. I don't know how long I'm going for, Harold.

HAROLD. I see.

Pause.

ELIZABETH. Or if I'm even coming back.

HAROLD. Funny that. I too must be something of a psychic. I was almost certain you were going to say that.

ELIZABETH. Something's happened.

HAROLD. That's a bit of an understatement isn't it?

Pause.

ELIZABETH. Charlotte said I can stay at hers for as long as I like.

HAROLD. Why don't you stay at ours? I'll speak to Mrs Greene and she can tidy the place up, it'll only take her a day or two.

ELIZABETH. I don't want to stay at your flat, Harold.

HAROLD. *Our* flat.

ELIZABETH. *Your* flat, Harold. It's yours. Everything is yours.

HAROLD. Anyway, your sister lives in two rooms and hasn't any money. You won't last a day.

ELIZABETH. I will.

HAROLD. In any case I'll speak to the man at Coutts and you can pass by later this week and take whatever money you need.

ELIZABETH. I shan't do that.

HAROLD. And then when you're feeling a little better I may come down myself for a few days, God knows it might do me some good.

ELIZABETH. You're not listening, Harold. You're not listening, you're not listening.

Pause.

I don't want the flat. I don't want the money. I *shall* manage, one way or another. Charlotte mentioned someone was looking for a French teacher.

HAROLD. Don't be absurd.

ELIZABETH. It's for young children, my French is good enough. And then we'll see. But I *shall* manage.

EILEEN *comes down the stairs carrying a couple of suitcases. She makes her way across the room and exits to the hallway.* ELIZABETH *only continues to speak when she is gone.*

Everything is yours. I sat in my room last night, after all that had happened and I looked at the wall and do you know what I thought?

HAROLD. What did you think, Elizabeth?

ELIZABETH. I thought, 'That wall is Harold's.' The bricks and
mortar that made this house. The fields beyond the window.
The way we are and the way we live. I sat there and I
thought, '*Everything is his*.' He has shaped this place in his
image, has stamped it with his mark. I stood up – I actually
started walking around the house – looking for myself. I
thought maybe I would – I *hoped* – that maybe I would find
myself somewhere. In a picture, an armchair, in the smallest
room. Something. But even when I looked in the mirror you
stared back at me.

HAROLD. What are you saying?

ELIZABETH. I am complicit. Not a victim but an accomplice.
It was the easier life you see. And it was seductive too. In the
beginning I worshipped all those qualities one admires in a
man. Determination and leadership. You frightened me
sometimes but even the fear I felt excited me. And I gave
myself to you and found my place in your shade and felt
some safety there. So I am as much to blame as you. I see
that now and I see something else too.

HAROLD. And what is that?

ELIZABETH. That you cower in the corner at the thought of
your own extinction. That you're threatened by the whispers
in the trees, by the shapes and shadows that dance at your feet
and more than anything else, by the true meaning of love.

Pause.

So you see I have to leave, Harold. I don't know where to –
oh, to my sister's yes, but then what? – what the future is I do
not know. But I think that if I stay here we shall both go mad.

She goes.

HAROLD *is left alone. He does not move. A few seconds
pass but he remains completely still*.

Then TERENCE *enters*.

TERENCE. Good morning.

HAROLD. Hello.

TERENCE. At last when I woke up this morning and looked out of the window I could see for miles and miles and remembered what a glorious part of the world this is.

HAROLD. It is, yes.

TERENCE. Where are the others?

HAROLD. They're walking around the garden.

TERENCE. Getting a bit of fresh air before the journey home.

HAROLD. Yes, they are.

TERENCE *walks over to where the coffee is and pours himself a cup.*

So you slept well.

TERENCE. Like a baby, yes. And no dreams or visions or anything of the kind.

HAROLD. Good. I think we've had enough of those.

TERENCE. Yes, quite enough.

He walks over to the window and looks out.

Mrs Pritchard is a little transformed. She looks as if some weight has been lifted from her shoulders.

HAROLD. Does she?

TERENCE. And I think it's a good thing that she's coming to London.

HAROLD. Is that what you think?

TERENCE. Returning, I mean.

HAROLD. Returning, yes.

TERENCE. To life.

Pause.

I have a confession to make.

HAROLD. What sort of a confession?

TERENCE. The night we arrived I was coming down to meet you. I got to the door but you were in a business meeting.

HAROLD. With my chief collier, yes.

TERENCE. I didn't want to interrupt. So I stood outside that door and overheard the conversation.

HAROLD. So you're an eavesdropper then?

TERENCE. In that instance, yes, I must admit it. My feet were rooted to the ground.

Pause.

His arguments, as you succinctly pointed out, were naive and unrealistic. Almost laughable really. He cajoled and begged, invoked pity, and then suggested a revolution of sorts. The ambition of the man was monumental even if his proposal was a little jejune.

HAROLD. Where are you going with this? I'm really not in the mood to discuss with you any of the dealings I have with my employees.

TERENCE. I do however think you misunderstood the gist of his point. I don't think he was denouncing technological advances, merely trying to suggest that the welfare of his colleagues – and their families – should be the driving motive.

HAROLD. Thank you for clarifying that.

TERENCE. Anyway, perhaps the unemployment is temporary. If we're lucky a little war and carnage will pick things up again. Isn't that what's necessary?

HAROLD. You're back to your normal self I see.

TERENCE. And then less than an hour after that I was witness to a different kind of pleading.

HAROLD. And what was that?

TERENCE. The pleading of your wife – her pleading for redemption.

He puts down his coffee cup.

I have something that I think you should have. It doesn't really belong to you but I think you should have it anyway.

He takes a small gold coin out of his pocket.

On my last morning on Mount Athos I swam to a tiny island a mile from the coast. Well, less of an island really, more of a rock with a little vegetation on it. I thought it was uninhabited but when I reached its shore I noticed there was a fire burning a few hundred feet inland, so fuelled by curiosity I made my way towards it. I came across a tiny wooden shack which was home to an alarming creature that bore a strong resemblance to a human being, only quite a bit more hirsute and shall we say malodorous.

HAROLD. Why are you telling me this?

TERENCE. At first I was a little frightened but then I realised that despite the mad glare in his eyes he was harmless, in fact completely benevolent. He was a monk who had been ejected from the monastery and labelled an apostate. His crime was to challenge those who mistake myth for reality. In somewhat fractured English he said to me, 'It is not the words of the story that matter, it is the meaning behind them.' Then he gave me this.

HAROLD. What is it?

TERENCE. A lucky coin. He said I was to always keep it on my person. He said it would help me make the right choices and lead me to them.

HAROLD. And you believed him.

TERENCE. Well, even though I thought he was a bit of a lunatic I rather liked him. So I took the coin and have had it ever since. Like a memory of my trip.

HAROLD. Good for you.

TERENCE. And as I was about to leave the island and swim back to the literalists he asked me a little about myself. I remember telling him that one day I would like to call myself an artist. And to that he said something that I shan't easily forget.

HAROLD. And what was that?

TERENCE. He said, 'When the world is separated into those who believe in nothing at all and those whose belief has made them blind it will be your duty to bridge the gap.'

Pause.

Anyway, the first night we arrived here, as I was undressing and getting ready for bed – well, wouldn't you know it – my lucky coin slipped out of my pocket and rolled to the edge of the room and disappeared under the carpet.

HAROLD. Did it?

TERENCE. That tiny slither of a gap between the edge of the carpet and the wall. Well, of course I couldn't let it disappear for ever without an effort to retrieve it and so I pulled up the carpet which surprisingly enough succumbed quite easily to my fingers, as if it had been lifted before, albeit many years ago.

HAROLD. Why are you telling me all this?

TERENCE. Do you know that the damn coin had gone one step further and fallen into the gap between the floorboards. Well, I wasn't going to give up that easily and so I tried to see if there was any way I could lift the floorboard and hey presto, it too surrendered to my attempt with hardly any resistance. I knew then that I wasn't the first.

HAROLD. So you got your coin back.

TERENCE. Yes, but more importantly it led me to this.

He takes out of his pocket a small, leather-bound book.

The handwriting I recognised immediately, that messy, childish scrawl that had written me many a letter. It brought tears to my eyes when I recognised it. This is the first page:

He reads from it.

'And so within these covers I offer you my secret thoughts, my secret hopes, my secret fears, my secret everythings in the hope that not only will you safeguard them but that in returning to your pages later on in life and reflecting on them you will help me to discover and understand something of where I've come from and suggest something of where I'm headed.' He's twelve years old, it's extraordinary.

And a few pages later: 'Betsy, God bless her, has bought a new hat that makes her look like a mad ostrich. "How are you going to fry us an egg in that?" I asked her and she laughed and laughed and laughed.'

And the very last entry: 'Father bought me chocolates from
Leeds to cheer me up now that the Averys have gone – my
favourite kind! Mother must have told him to because she
knows I'm sad and I miss Terence already, he is the best
friend I've ever known and he understands me more than any
other. I shall now go and pick some heather for Mother
because she loves it so and then set off on an adventure. I
shall head east for the first time, and go far, maybe get as far
as Bracken Moor.'

Pause. TERENCE *hands him the diary.*

Take it. You will learn things about your son and his
indomitable, courageous spirit.

HAROLD. A piece of theatre then. An artifice, a melodrama.

TERENCE. Performed with dedication though.

HAROLD *hits him hard across the face.* TERENCE *reels.*

Well, no surprises there. The language of force, the only one
you know.

HAROLD. What kind of an animal are you?

TERENCE. A human being, sir.

HAROLD. A lying dog, a charlatan.

TERENCE. Don't speak of lying and of lies, your life is made
of them.

HAROLD. I warn you.

TERENCE. No doubt you've sat in smoke-filled rooms with
men that mirror you in every way, brandishing words like
'enterprise' and 'meritocracy' with passionate conviction.
These words ring hollow in your mouth. Perhaps you've also
invoked Darwin as an excuse for everything you are, citing
him as proof that your way is the best. But now, for once,
you listen to someone else.

HAROLD *takes him by the lapels and drags him across the
room, pinning him against the wall as if to silence him. But*
TERENCE *will not be silenced.*

You know nothing of the truth. This house is built on the sweat of others and the way you think the coal your own is an affront to God and every living being. The irrationality is yours: you can not own the coal any more than you can own the waters that lap our shores or the sky that rages above our heads. None of it is yours to own and the people who have given their lives to wrench it from the earth have more a right to it than you do.

HAROLD *throws him on the floor.*

Think on that before you throw them to the dogs.

He stands just as ELIZABETH, VANESSA *and* GEOFFREY *walk into the room.*

GEOFFREY. Damn cold out there.

VANESSA. I'm afraid our stroll has been cut short.

GEOFFREY. More's the pity.

ELIZABETH. Mr McLean thinks we should be heading off a little earlier than he first suggested. He said there's a possibility of snow this afternoon.

VANESSA. You wouldn't think so looking at that blue sky.

ELIZABETH. So he's helping Eileen load the car.

VANESSA. Oh, I do hope the trains will be on time.

GEOFFREY. Are you all right, old man? You look as if you've seen a ghost.

ELIZABETH. Harold?

VANESSA. Terence, what's the matter? Are you two all right?

TERENCE. We're fine. Aren't we, Mr Pritchard?

Pause.

HAROLD. Yes. Yes. Yes, we're fine.

ELIZABETH (*pointing to the diary*). What's that you're holding, Harold?

HAROLD. This?

Pause.

Oh, this. It's a book of… it's accounts. Nothing important.

Pause.

VANESSA. Well, Harold, now that Elizabeth has decided to make a journey south perhaps you should consider it as well. We look forward to having you for dinner at some point before the spring. You can't stay up here for ever, can you?

GEOFFREY. I'll take you to the club, old boy, and we can misbehave.

VANESSA. You're far too old to misbehave, you'll just look ridiculous.

GEOFFREY. Thank you for having us anyway. I wish I could say it's been a pleasure but I'd be lying through my teeth.

VANESSA. And don't you worry, we'll keep an eye on her and make sure no harm comes to her and send her back fresh as a daisy and with lots of beautiful new clothes. God knows, maybe even with pineapple curtains and Hubert De Carcasson in tow.

GEOFFREY. What on earth are you babbling on about?

VANESSA. Never you mind. Goodbye, Harold.

She kisses him.

HAROLD. Goodbye, Vanessa. Goodbye, Geoffrey.

TERENCE (*stretching his hand out for* HAROLD *to shake*). Goodbye, sir. And thank you for your kindness.

HAROLD *looks at his hand but does not take it for some time. Eventually, he shakes it.*

VANESSA, GEOFFREY *and* TERENCE *leave.*

ELIZABETH. I shall call you when I arrive.

HAROLD. Yes.

Pause.

ELIZABETH. He's quite an extraordinary boy isn't he?

HAROLD. Extraordinary, yes.

ELIZABETH. I don't know what he is. He has a gift. Or maybe a curse, God knows. I was trying to come up with the right word. Is he a visionary, I thought? A seer? A shaman?

HAROLD. Quite extraordinary.

ELIZABETH. And when he did what he did – lived those last, terrible moments of our Edgar something happened, didn't it. He went there, all the way, became him, felt his fear, his anguish.

Pause.

Perhaps that's what I mean by love. To be able to do that. To feel the pain of others as if it is your own. Maybe that's all it is. An act of imagination.

She kisses him. She makes her way to the door but stops when he begins to speak. He speaks slowly and in a confused way, as if he is talking mostly to himself, trying to solve some half-forgotten problem.

HAROLD. Elizabeth. I am not. What I mean to say is. Not a bad man, Elizabeth, not a bad man. My father. His father before him. It isn't easy is what I think I'm trying to say. And everything we have, the roof above our head, the food on our table, the walls that keep us warm, Elizabeth – the ones you say are mine. Sometimes I feel as if the world will fall apart if I cease to carry it on my shoulders.

ELIZABETH. Will it, Harold?

She goes.

HAROLD. Edgar. My boy. My angel.

And suddenly, for a second, it looks as if he'll break. His body looks as if it might collapse under the weight of this new emotion, he begins to make a sound of unbearable pain. But just as quickly, he suppresses it.

EILEEN *enters.*

EILEEN. Excuse me, sir, Mr Bailey is here to see you.

HAROLD. Send him in.

EILEEN. Yes, sir. Will you be wanting any more coffee, sir?

HAROLD. No, thank you, Eileen.

EILEEN. Shall I clear it all away, sir?

HAROLD. Do that.

She starts to clear up the coffee cups.

EILEEN. Sir, it's my day off today.

HAROLD. Is it indeed?

EILEEN. I know things have changed, sir, what with Mrs
   Pritchard leaving for London so unexpectedly but will it be
   all right if I still go into the village to see my mother? I'll be
   back before dinner.

HAROLD. Do that.

EILEEN. So I shall tell Mr Bailey he can come through, sir, and
   then after that I'll be off. Are you sure you'll be all right on
   your own, sir?

HAROLD. We'll have to wait and see.

EILEEN *is slightly confused by his answer but she shrugs it
   off and goes.* HAROLD *is left alone. He remains still. A few
   seconds later,* JOHN *enters.*

JOHN. Good morning, sir.

HAROLD. Good morning, Mr Bailey.

JOHN. I dropped by yesterday but at the wrong time and so I've
   returned today.

HAROLD. What is it, Mr Bailey?

JOHN. The papers have come through, sir.

HAROLD. What papers?

JOHN. For you to sign, sir, for the purchase and delivery of the
   new machinery from America.

HAROLD. I see.

JOHN. Mr Milson asked me to tell you that if we send them off by tomorrow morning there's every likelihood the machines will get here before the end of the year.

HAROLD. That's good.

JOHN. That means that the installation can begin in the first week of January and that they'll be in full operation by the middle of the same month. The work shouldn't take longer than a couple of weeks at most if everything runs like clockwork.

HAROLD. Yes.

JOHN. But you need to sign them, sir.

HAROLD. Of course.

Pause.

Well, bring them here then and I'll sign.

JOHN. Yes, sir.

JOHN takes the papers over to him. HAROLD places them on the table in front of him and takes his pen out of his pocket. He starts skimming through the documents.

And so Ramshaw Drift is to close, sir.

HAROLD. As arranged, yes.

JOHN. And those one hundred and forty men and their families –

HAROLD. Please refrain, Mr Bailey. Please.

JOHN. Yes, sir.

HAROLD signs all the documents. He puts his pen back into his pocket and hands the papers back to JOHN. He takes them and starts to walk towards the door. But HAROLD stops him. He talks to JOHN but does not turn to look at him. Instead he is staring forwards.

HAROLD. I am running a business, Mr Bailey. I am running a business.

JOHN *does not answer. He leaves the room, closing the door behind him.*

HAROLD *is left alone. He stares ahead. A few seconds pass like this.*

Then suddenly, EDGAR *appears out of nowhere behind him. He is covered in soil and dirt, as if he has been underground for a long time. When he speaks his voice is terrible, as if its source is down deep in the ground, miles below the surface, in the bowels of the earth.*

EDGAR. Father.

Blackout.

The End.

A Nick Hern Book

Bracken Moor first published in Great Britain as a paperback original in 2013 by Nick Hern Books Limited, The Glasshouse, 49a Goldhawk Road, London W12 8QP, in association with Shared Experience and the Tricycle Theatre, London

Bracken Moor copyright © 2013 Alexi Kaye Campbell

Alexi Kaye Campbell has asserted his right to be identified as the author of this work

Tricycle Theatre branding and cover artwork by aka (www.akauk.com)
Cover design by Ned Hoste, 2H

Typeset by Nick Hern Books, London
Printed and bound by CPI Group (UK) Ltd, Croydon, CR0 4YY

A CIP catalogue record for this book is available from the British Library

ISBN   978 1 84842 332 9